SOCIAL ANXIETY

Feel Confident in a Crowd, on a Date, and at Work Gatherings by Identifying Personal Triggers, Diffusing High Stress Thoughts, and Relaxing Into True Comfort, Ease and Confidence

JANE KENNEDY

© **Copyright 2024 - All rights reserved.**

The content contained within this book may not be reproduced, duplicated or transmitted without direct written permission from the author or the publisher.

Under no circumstances will any blame or legal responsibility be held against the publisher, or author, for any damages, reparation, or monetary loss due to the information contained within this book, either directly or indirectly.

Legal Notice:

This book is copyright protected. It is only for personal use. You cannot amend, distribute, sell, use, quote or paraphrase any part, or the content within this book, without the consent of the author or publisher.

Disclaimer Notice:

Please note the information contained within this document is for educational and entertainment purposes only. All effort has been executed to present accurate, up to date, reliable, complete information. No warranties of any kind are declared or implied. Readers acknowledge that the author is not engaged in the rendering of legal, financial, medical or professional advice. The content within this book has been derived from various sources. Please consult a licensed professional before attempting any techniques outlined in this book.

By reading this document, the reader agrees that under no circumstances is the author responsible for any losses, direct or indirect, that are incurred as a result of the use of the information contained within this document, including, but not limited to, errors, omissions, or inaccuracies.

TABLE OF CONTENTS

Introduction 1

Chapter 1 5

Understanding Social Anxiety: Foundations 5

    Defining Social Anxiety 6

    Common Symptoms and Identifying Signs 8

        Root Causes and Contributing Factors 11

        Impact On Daily Life and Relationships 12

Chapter 2 16

The Science Behind Social Anxiety 16

    Role of Brain Chemistry 17

    Understanding the Fight-or-Flight Response 19

        Physical Symptoms of Social Anxiety 19

        Techniques for Managing Physical Symptoms ... 20

        Combining Techniques for Greater Effectiveness ... 22

        Long-Term Benefits 22

    Genetic Predispositions 23

    Influence of Past Experiences and Trauma 24

Chapter 3 29

Identifying Your Triggers 29

    Types of Social Situations That Trigger Anxiety 30

    Personal Reflection Exercises 32

    Documenting Anxious Moments 34

    Pattern Recognition and Common Themes 36

Chapter 4 40
Cognitive-Behavioral Techniques 40

Challenging Negative Thoughts 41

Exposure Therapy Basics 43

Decatastrophizing Techniques 45

Developing a Growth Mindset 46

Chapter 5 50
Mindfulness and Relaxation Strategies 50

Breathing Exercises 51

    Breathing Techniques for Anxiety Reduction 51

    Integrating These Techniques 54

Guided Meditation Practices 54

Progressive Muscle Relaxation 56

    Understanding PMR 56

    Step-by-Step PMR Guide 57

    Integrating PMR Into Daily Life 58

    Benefits of PMR 59

Mindful Awareness in Social Settings 59

Chapter 6 63
Building Confidence Through Practice 63

Setting Achievable Goals 64

Incremental Success 66

Gradual Exposure to Feared Situations 68

    Exposure Hierarchy 69

    Visualization Techniques 69

    Reflecting Through Journaling 70

    Peer Support 70

    Seeking Feedback and Improvement 70

    Celebrating Small Victories 72

Chapter 7 76

Improving Communication Skills 76

    Active Listening Techniques 77

    Effective Verbal Communication Strategies 79

        Clarity and Conciseness 79

        Using Open-Ended Questions 80

        Practicing Tone and Pace 80

        Emphasizing Storytelling 81

    Non-Verbal Communication Cues 81

    Overcoming Fear of Public Speaking 84

Chapter 8 87

Support Systems and Professional Help 87

    Building a Supportive Network 88

    Role of Therapy and Counseling 89

    Group Therapy Benefits 91

    Utilizing Online Resources and Support Groups 94

Chapter 9 97

Real-Life Success Stories 97

    Case Study: Sarah's Journey 98

    Interview With a Therapist 101

        Therapist's Approach 101

        Advice for Overcoming Anxiety 103

    Success Story Compilation 104

Lessons Learned From Others' Experiences 106

Chapter 10 110

Maintaining Progress and Looking Forward 110

Reflection On Personal Growth 111

Setting Long-Term Goals...113

Conclusion..117

References 120

INTRODUCTION

If you've ever felt your heart race in a crowded room or wished you could disappear during a dinner party, you're not alone. Millions face the silent battle of social anxiety, feeling trapped in their own fears. This book is for you. It's also for mental health professionals seeking to better support their clients and anyone interested in personal development wanting to enhance their social skills and overall emotional well-being.

In a world that values social interaction and connection, experiencing social anxiety can feel like a heavy burden. Those moments of intense fear and self-doubt, when all eyes seem to be on you, are not just fleeting discomforts. They are experiences shared by countless individuals who, like you, often find themselves avoiding social situations out of sheer apprehension. Social anxiety goes beyond mere shyness; it's an overwhelming fear that disrupts daily life, making ordinary interactions feel like insurmountable challenges.

Imagine standing at a gathering, your mind racing with thoughts of judgment, fear gripping your chest, making it hard to breathe. You worry about saying the wrong thing, appearing awkward, or being scrutinized by others. These feelings are not figments of your imagination; they are part of a real and debilitating condition called social anxiety. Understanding this is crucial because recognizing the nature of your struggles is the first step toward overcoming them.

Social anxiety can be understood as an overwhelming fear of social interactions, leading to avoidance and significant distress. It's more than feeling shy or being introverted—it's a profound unease that can limit your life's possibilities. When social anxiety takes hold, it can affect various aspects of life, from personal relationships to professional opportunities, leaving many feeling isolated and misunderstood.

The significance of awareness cannot be overstated. Awareness is your first ally in the journey to break free from the chains of social anxiety. Understanding the origins of your fears marks the initial courageous step toward regaining control over your life and confidence. Awareness leads to transformation, turning self-doubt into self-assurance and fear into resilience.

This book aims to provide a comprehensive guide to understanding and managing social anxiety. In the chapters that follow, you will uncover powerful techniques, real-life stories, and actionable strategies designed to equip you with the skills needed to transform anxiety into confidence. You will learn about cognitive-behavioral approaches, mindfulness practices, and other evidence-based methods that have helped many navigate similar paths successfully.

We will explore how social anxiety manifests differently in each person, acknowledging that your experience is unique. Some might dread speaking in public, while others may avoid small talk at a gathering. The spectrum of social anxiety varies widely, but the core impacts—fear, avoidance, and distress—are common threads that bind those affected.

One of the first steps on this journey is to highlight the importance of recognizing and understanding social anxiety. t. Bringing attention to this frequently concealed struggle opens the door to healing and growth. Anxiety does not define you. Instead, increased awareness provides you with the tools to understand and manage it, fostering a sense of empowerment.

As you delve deeper into this book, you'll discover practical solutions tailored to address your specific needs and preferences. From learning to navigate conversations with ease to building resilience in the face of social challenges, each chapter is designed to offer insights and techniques that can make a tangible difference in your life.

You'll read inspiring stories of individuals who have successfully managed their social anxiety, offering hope and validation. Their journeys reflect the possibility of change and the power of persistence. Their experiences serve as a reminder that it is possible to move from a place of fear to one of confidence and fulfillment.

For mental health professionals, this book serves as a valuable resource to better support clients dealing with social anxiety. Through evidence-based strategies and therapeutic interventions, therapists, counselors, and coaches can empower their clients to develop healthier coping mechanisms and improve their quality of life.

For those interested in personal development, the insights gained from this book can enrich your understanding of human behavior and emotional well-being. Enhancing your social skills not only benefits your personal relationships but also contributes to professional success and overall happiness.

Your journey to a more fulfilling social life begins now. In the chapters ahead, you will find a blend of scientific research, practical advice, and compassionate guidance. Each section is crafted to provide clarity, support, and motivation, helping you navigate the complexities of social anxiety with greater ease.

As you embark on this transformative journey, remember that progress may take time, and that's okay. Every small step forward is a victory worth celebrating. With patience, persistence, and the right strategies, you can break free from the grip of social anxiety and embrace a life filled with meaningful connections and opportunities.

Together, we will explore the path to overcoming social anxiety, empowering you to face social situations with newfound confidence. This book is your companion, offering insights, tools, and encouragement every step of the way. Your story is important, and your journey matters. Let's begin this adventure toward a brighter, more connected future.

CHAPTER 1

Understanding Social Anxiety: Foundations

Understanding social anxiety is essential for anyone looking to navigate the complexities of social interactions with greater ease. Social anxiety isn't just about feeling nervous in certain situations; it's a deep-seated fear that can affect various aspects of one's daily life, leading to avoidance behaviors and significant emotional distress. Delving into this subject allows readers to gain valuable insights into the nature of social anxiety, distinguishing it from common nervousness or shyness.

This chapter will explore the foundational elements of social anxiety, including its definition, symptoms, and underlying causes. Readers will learn how to identify the signs of social anxiety and understand the factors that contribute to its development. This knowledge aims to foster awareness and empathy, making it easier for individuals and professionals to address and manage social anxiety effectively. Through an in-depth examination of these components, we aim to lay the groundwork for a comprehensive understanding of social anxiety, paving the way for practical solutions and improved quality of life.

Defining Social Anxiety

Understanding social anxiety is fundamental for those affected by it and for professionals who support them. Social anxiety is a persistent and sometimes overwhelming fear of social situations where one feels they may be scrutinized or judged negatively. This fear can cause significant distress and impairment in daily functioning, making it crucial to identify and understand its nature.

Unlike the occasional nervousness that many people experience before public speaking or meeting new people, social anxiety is more intense and chronic. Individuals with social anxiety often worry excessively about being embarrassed or negatively evaluated by others. This anxiety can manifest in various situations, such as speaking in front of a group, eating in public, or even engaging in small talk. The constant fear of humiliation or judgment can lead to avoidance behaviors, significantly impacting one's personal and professional life.

A common misconception is that social anxiety is merely an extreme form of shyness. Shyness is generally characterized by mild discomfort or awkwardness in social settings, which usually diminishes over time as one becomes more familiar with the situation. On the other hand, social anxiety involves a more profound level of fear and avoidance that does not easily subside. Understanding this distinction is essential, as it helps individuals recognize whether their experiences go beyond typical shyness and might require further attention and intervention.

Moreover, it's important to dispel the belief that social anxiety equates to being introverted. Introversion is a personality trait where individuals tend to feel more energized by solitary activities rather than social interactions. Introverts can enjoy and perform well in social settings without experiencing the debilitating fear characteristic of social anxiety. Distinguishing social anxiety from introversion helps foster self-awareness and prevents misunderstandings that might discourage someone from seeking help.

Recognizing social anxiety as a legitimate mental health issue is crucial for several reasons. Firstly, it validates the experiences of those suffering from it, acknowledging that their fears are real and worthy of attention. Secondly, it encourages a more empathetic response from friends, family, and colleagues, fostering a supportive environment. Lastly, understanding that social anxiety is a treatable condition can motivate individuals to seek professional help, improving their quality of life.

Becoming aware is the crucial first step in overcoming social anxiety. Educating oneself about the symptoms and underlying mechanisms of this condition can make a significant difference. It enables individuals to articulate their experiences more accurately, reducing feelings of isolation and helplessness. For instance, understanding that physical symptoms like sweating, trembling, and rapid heartbeat are common responses to social anxiety can normalize these experiences, making them less intimidating.

Differentiating between normal nervousness and social anxiety can empower individuals to take appropriate action. While occasional nervousness might be managed through simple relaxation techniques or gradual exposure to feared situations, social anxiety often requires a more structured approach. Cognitive-behavioral therapy (CBT) is one of the most effective treatments, focusing on identifying and challenging negative thought patterns and gradually exposing individuals to feared social situations in a controlled manner. Acknowledging the need for treatment allows individuals to embark on a journey toward improved social functioning and overall well-being.

It's also vital to address the stigma surrounding mental health issues, including social anxiety. Many people hesitate to seek help due to fear of being labeled or misunderstood. Raising awareness on social anxiety can counteract these stigmas, promoting a culture where seeking help is seen as a positive and proactive step. Encouraging open conversations about mental health and sharing personal stories of coping and recovery can further reduce the barriers to seeking support.

In addition to therapy, there are various strategies individuals can employ to manage social anxiety in their daily lives. These include practicing mindfulness and relaxation techniques, setting realistic goals, and gradually facing feared situations. Building a strong support network of understanding friends, family, or support groups can also provide valuable encouragement and companionship.

Employing practical solutions tailored to one's specific needs is crucial for managing social anxiety effectively. For example, preparing for social interactions in advance, such as planning conversation topics or practicing assertiveness skills, can boost confidence and reduce anxiety. Understanding that progress may be gradual and setbacks are a natural part of the process can help maintain motivation and resilience.

Understanding the link between mental and physical health is essential. Regular exercise, adequate sleep, and a balanced diet can enhance overall well-being and help reduce anxiety levels. Incorporating these lifestyle changes into one's routine can complement therapeutic interventions, providing a comprehensive approach to managing social anxiety.

Common Symptoms and Identifying Signs

Understanding the symptoms of social anxiety is crucial for readers who may be experiencing it themselves or for professionals assisting clients with this condition. Recognizing and understanding these symptoms can lead to early intervention and more effective management strategies.

To start, examining the emotional symptoms of social anxiety lays the groundwork for a deeper understanding. Individuals often experience intense feelings of fear, dread, and embarrassment in social situations. These emotions are persistent and can significantly affect one's quality of life. For example, a person might feel overwhelming dread before attending a social event, fearing judgment or ridicule from others. This ongoing emotional distress can hinder participation in everyday activities and lead to social withdrawal. Recognizing these feelings as part of social anxiety, rather than personal failings, is crucial for taking proactive steps toward improvement.

Next, outlining the physical symptoms associated with social anxiety helps to normalize these responses and reduce the stigma surrounding the condition. Common physical manifestations include sweating, trembling, and an increased heart rate. For instance, someone with social anxiety might experience sweaty palms and a shaky voice when speaking in front of a group. The racing heart can make them feel faint or out of control. Understanding that these physical reactions are typical and not indicative of a severe medical issue can reassure individuals and encourage them to seek appropriate help. Knowing that others have similar experiences can also foster a sense of belonging and lessen feelings of isolation.

The cognitive symptoms of social anxiety involve negative thought patterns and obsessive worries. People often harbor irrational fears about being judged, embarrassed, or rejected by others. They might constantly think, *I will say something stupid,* or *Everyone will think I am boring.* These intrusive thoughts create a cycle of anxiety that can be difficult to break. However, managing these thought patterns with healthier thinking techniques is possible. Cognitive-behavioral therapy (CBT) is one effective approach. It helps individuals identify and challenge their negative beliefs, replacing them with more realistic and positive ones. For example, instead of thinking, *I will embarrass myself,* a person could train themselves to think, *It's okay if I make a mistake; everyone does sometimes.*

Behavioral symptoms manifest as avoidance behaviors. Avoidance is a significant barrier to progress because it prevents individuals from facing their fears and gaining confidence in social settings. For example, someone with social anxiety might avoid parties, meetings, or even simple interactions like making a phone call. While avoidance may provide temporary relief, it ultimately reinforces anxiety and maintains the cycle of fear. Breaking free from avoidance behaviors involves gradually exposing oneself to feared situations in a controlled manner. Starting with less intimidating scenarios and progressively tackling more challenging ones can build resilience and reduce anxiety over time.

Guidelines for managing these symptoms effectively include seeking professional help, practicing self-care, and engaging in gradual exposure to anxiety-provoking situations. Professional help from therapists who specialize in social anxiety can be invaluable. Therapists can offer tailored strategies such as CBT to address specific thought patterns and behaviors. Practicing self-care is equally important. Regular exercise, proper nutrition, adequate sleep, and mindfulness practices can all contribute to overall well-being and stress reduction. Mindfulness, in particular, helps individuals stay present and reduces the focus on anxious thoughts about the past or future.

Gradual exposure to social situations, a technique used in behavioral therapies, can desensitize individuals to their fears. For instance, starting with small social tasks like making eye contact with strangers or participating in brief conversations can serve as stepping stones toward larger goals. Over time, these small achievements build confidence and lessen the grip of social anxiety. Support groups can also offer a nurturing environment where individuals share experiences and coping strategies, promoting mutual encouragement and understanding.

Additionally, it is essential to create a supportive network of friends and family who understand the challenges faced by those with social anxiety. Open communication about one's struggles can foster empathy and support. Encouraging loved ones to accompany individuals to social events or practice social skills together can further bolster confidence and motivation.

Educating people about the symptoms, causes, and treatment options for social anxiety is crucial for demystifying the condition. A thorough understanding of how social anxiety manifests and impacts daily life benefits both those who experience it and their support networks. By raising awareness and reducing stigma, society can foster a more inclusive and supportive environment for those dealing with social anxiety.

Root Causes and Contributing Factors

Understanding the underlying causes of social anxiety is essential for anyone looking to manage it effectively. This exploration begins with an examination of how life experiences and personality traits contribute to social anxiety, which fosters self-awareness. Events from childhood, adolescence, or even adulthood can significantly impact one's social comfort levels. For instance, negative experiences such as bullying, rejection, or constant criticism may ingrain a fear of social situations. Personality traits, such as introversion or perfectionism, can further exacerbate this unease. Recognizing these factors allows individuals to better understand why they feel anxious in social scenarios and begin addressing these root causes.

Another significant factor in the development and maintenance of social anxiety is upbringing. The way one is raised, along with societal pressures and cultural norms, profoundly affects self-worth and social performance. In many cultures, high expectations for social behavior and success can create immense pressure. Children who grow up in environments that emphasize public approval or harshly criticize social missteps may internalize these attitudes, linking their self-worth directly to their social performance. Understanding and acknowledging these influences can help individuals separate their self-esteem from their social prowess, thereby reducing the intensity of social anxiety.

Closely related to upbringing and cultural norms is the role of Social Learning Theory in shaping social behaviors and anxieties. According to this theory, much of our behavior is learned through observing and imitating others. If a child frequently observes parents or peers displaying anxious behaviors in social settings, they are likely to adopt these patterns themselves. Similarly, observing confident and relaxed social interactions can have a positive influence. Becoming aware of the behaviors we've unconsciously mimicked allows us to start consciously choosing more constructive ways of interacting socially.

Lastly, understanding the cyclical nature of anxiety and avoidance is crucial for breaking free from the grip of social anxiety. When individuals experience anxiety in social situations, their natural response is often to avoid these situations altogether. While this avoidance provides temporary relief, it reinforces the anxiety in the long run, creating a destructive cycle. Each avoided event strengthens the belief that social situations are dangerous, making it increasingly difficult to face them in the future. Recognizing this cycle is the first step toward disrupting it. Gradually exposing oneself to social situations and challenging anxious thoughts can help individuals slowly build confidence and reduce their anxiety over time.

Impact On Daily Life and Relationships

Social anxiety is a condition that significantly affects various facets of life, making it crucial to address the disorder for overall well-being and fulfillment. Understanding how social anxiety hinders the formation and maintenance of friendships is vital in creating a sense of urgency for change. Friendships are essential to human life, providing emotional support, companionship, and a deep sense of belonging. However, individuals with social anxiety often struggle to engage in social interactions due to an intense fear of being judged or humiliated. This fear leads to avoidance behaviors, such as declining social invitations or feeling excessively anxious at gatherings, making it challenging to form new connections.

For instance, take Sarah, who struggles with severe social anxiety. She finds attending social events challenging due to her fear of being scrutinized by others. This persistent worry stops her from initiating conversations, resulting in feelings of isolation and loneliness. Understanding Sarah's experience highlights the importance of addressing social anxiety to foster and maintain meaningful relationships. When individuals recognize their social anxiety and seek help, they become better equipped to form connections, thereby strengthening their social support network and enhancing their quality of life.

Challenges in the workplace due to social anxiety further emphasize the need for developing coping mechanisms. The workplace is an environment where social interactions are inevitable, whether it's participating in meetings, collaborating with colleagues, or giving presentations. For those with social anxiety, these situations can be overwhelmingly stressful, hindering their professional growth and productivity.

Consider John, who has social anxiety and works in a corporate environment. He experiences constant dread when asked to speak during team meetings, fearing negative judgment from his peers. Consequently, he often stays silent, which might be misunderstood as disinterest or lack of confidence. To address these challenges, John and others in similar situations can benefit from strategies like cognitive-behavioral techniques to manage their anxiety, gradual exposure to social situations to build confidence, and seeking support from mental health professionals. Developing effective coping mechanisms improves workplace performance and contributes to a healthier work environment.

Social anxiety's interference with everyday tasks underscores the necessity of adopting healthier coping strategies. Daily activities, such as grocery shopping, attending appointments, or even making phone calls, can be daunting for someone with social anxiety. These routine tasks, typically considered mundane, become sources of significant stress, impacting an individual's ability to function effectively in their daily life.

For example, Emma experiences social anxiety that makes it difficult for her to perform everyday tasks. She avoids going to busy places like supermarkets for fear of interacting with strangers. Instead, she relies on online shopping, which, while convenient, limits her opportunities for social interaction and reinforces her anxiety. Recognizing the impact of social anxiety on daily activities ensures individuals can seek methods to better manage these fears of social interactions. Techniques such as mindfulness practices, relaxation exercises, and gradually confronting feared situations can help reduce anxiety and improve overall functioning in daily life.

Lastly, emphasizing the long-term emotional and psychological effects of social anxiety reinforces the urgent need to seek help. Social anxiety doesn't just affect immediate interactions; its consequences can extend far into one's mental health and emotional well-being. Persistent anxiety can lead to chronic stress, depression, and a diminished sense of self-worth. These long-term effects highlight the critical importance of addressing social anxiety early to prevent more severe mental health issues.

Consider Mark, who has struggled with social anxiety for years without seeking help. Over time, his constant fear of social rejection has led to feelings of hopelessness and depression. He isolates himself from social interactions, further exacerbating his anxiety and contributing to a cycle of negative emotions. Focusing on the potential long-term effects helps to grasp the severity of social anxiety and underscores the importance of seeking professional support. Mental health interventions, such as therapy and medication, can significantly improve an individual's quality of life by reducing symptoms and providing tools to manage anxiety effectively.

In this chapter, we've established a foundational understanding of social anxiety by examining its definition, symptoms, and causes. We explored how social anxiety extends beyond simple nervousness or shyness, significantly impacting one's ability to participate in daily social interactions. By acknowledging the emotional, physical, and cognitive symptoms, individuals can more effectively recognize their experiences and begin the journey toward seeking help. Additionally, our discussion emphasized the important role that upbringing, cultural norms, and social learning play in the development of social anxiety, offering insights into the underlying causes of this condition.

Recognizing the multifaceted impact of social anxiety on daily life and relationships highlights the necessity of addressing it thoroughly. Social anxiety obstructs personal and professional interactions and affects overall well-being and mental health. By understanding these challenges, both those who experience social anxiety and those who support them can create a more empathetic environment and encourage proactive steps toward management and recovery. With increased awareness and suitable interventions, such as cognitive-behavioral therapy and gradual exposure, individuals can begin to overcome the cycle of fear and avoidance, ultimately enhancing their quality of life.

CHAPTER 2
The Science Behind Social Anxiety

Social anxiety is intricately linked to the complex interplay of various psychological and physiological mechanisms. This chapter delves into the nuanced relationships between brain chemistry, genetic predispositions, and the body's stress response system, all of which contribute to the development and persistence of social anxiety. Examining these underlying processes provides a comprehensive understanding of why some individuals experience heightened anxiety in social situations.

We will examine how neurotransmitters such as serotonin, dopamine, and norepinephrine influence mood regulation and stress responses, emphasizing the significant effects of chemical imbalances on social interactions. The chapter will also cover the role of cortisol and the genetic factors that impact these biochemical pathways. By exploring how inherited traits and chronic stress interact with brain chemistry, we aim to provide insights into personalized treatments based on recent advancements in neuroscience and genetics. This exploration will offer readers a deeper understanding of the biological foundations of social anxiety, leading to a more empathetic and informed approach to managing the condition.

Role of Brain Chemistry

The complex interplay of chemicals in our brain greatly affects how we perceive and engage with the world, especially in social settings. Neurotransmitters such as serotonin, dopamine, and norepinephrine, play a central role in this process. These chemical messengers regulate mood, emotions, and our physiological responses to stress. An imbalance in these neurotransmitters can lead to increased feelings of anxiety, particularly in social situations.

Serotonin, often dubbed the "feel-good" neurotransmitter, plays a pivotal role in mood regulation and social behavior. Adequate levels of serotonin contribute to feelings of well-being and happiness. However, when serotonin levels drop, individuals may experience increased anxiety, depression, and emotional instability. The deficiency of serotonin can make social interactions incredibly daunting, leading to an overwhelming fear of judgment or rejection.

Dopamine is another key player in the realm of mood and anxiety. This neurotransmitter is essential for reward processing and motivation. When dopamine levels are balanced, we feel pleasure and satisfaction from social interactions and achievements. Conversely, low dopamine levels can result in diminished motivation and pleasure, causing social engagements to feel less rewarding and more intimidating. The lack of positive reinforcement from social activities can lead to avoidance behaviors, further entrenching social anxiety.

Norepinephrine, also known as noradrenaline, functions as both a hormone and a neurotransmitter. It is integral to the body's "fight-or-flight" response, which prepares us to react to perceived threats. Elevated levels of norepinephrine can make individuals hyper-vigilant and overly sensitive to social cues, interpreting neutral or benign interactions as threatening. This heightened state of alertness can cause physical symptoms such as sweating, trembling, or an accelerated heart rate during social encounters, exacerbating feelings of anxiety.

In addition to these neurotransmitters, cortisol, a stress hormone, plays a significant role in social anxiety. When faced with stress, the body releases cortisol to help manage the situation. However, chronic stress leads to consistently high levels of cortisol, which increases sensitivity to social threats. This heightened sensitivity makes it difficult to cope with social interactions, as the individual perceives them as more threatening than they truly are. Elevated cortisol levels can, therefore, create a feedback loop, perpetuating the cycle of social anxiety.

Beyond the immediate biochemical reactions, genetic predispositions also play a crucial role in influencing neurotransmitter functions and the development of social anxiety. Studies have shown that individuals with a family history of anxiety disorders are more likely to experience similar conditions themselves. This hereditary pattern indicates that genetic factors can affect how neurotransmitters function, predisposing some individuals to imbalances that heighten social anxiety.

Understanding the genetic component provides valuable insights into why certain individuals are more susceptible to social anxiety. It helps destigmatize the condition by framing it as a biological issue rather than a character flaw. Recognizing the hereditary aspect also opens up possibilities for more personalized treatment approaches. For instance, if a person knows they have a genetic predisposition to neurotransmitter imbalances, they might benefit from early interventions aimed at mitigating the risk of developing severe social anxiety.

As researchers delve deeper into the complexities of brain chemistry, new avenues for treatment emerge. Emerging research on neurotransmitter imbalances offers hope for innovative therapies targeting these specific chemical discrepancies. For instance, selective serotonin reuptake inhibitors (SSRIs) are commonly prescribed to manage anxiety and depression by boosting serotonin levels in the brain. Likewise, other medications and therapeutic methods aimed at adjusting dopamine and norepinephrine levels are being investigated to offer a more thorough approach to managing social anxiety.

Moreover, advancements in neuroscience and genetics hold promise for creating highly targeted treatments. Techniques like pharmacogenomics—the study of how genes affect a person's response to drugs—can lead to personalized medication plans that are more effective and have fewer side effects. Tailoring treatments to an individual's specific genetic makeup and neurotransmitter profile allows healthcare providers to offer more precise and effective relief from social anxiety.

Understanding the Fight-or-Flight Response

The physiological response underlying social anxiety often begins with the fight-or-flight mechanism, an adaptive evolutionary process designed to prepare the body for immediate danger. While this response is crucial in life-threatening situations, it can become maladaptive when triggered by social scenarios. For instance, during a public speech or a social gathering, the body may perceive these situations as threats, leading to the activation of the fight-or-flight response.

Physical Symptoms of Social Anxiety

When the fight-or-flight response is activated, it triggers several physical symptoms:

1. **Increased Heart Rate**
    - The heart beats faster to pump more blood to muscles, preparing the body for action.
    - This can make individuals feel jittery or experience palpitations, especially in social settings.
2. **Perspiration**
    - The body produces sweat to cool down the muscles and regulate temperature.

- Excessive sweating, especially in the palms or underarms, can be particularly distressing during social interactions.

3. **Blushing**
    - Blood vessels in the face dilate, causing visible redness.
    - Blushing can be embarrassing and heightens feelings of self-consciousness.

4. **Muscle Tension**
    - Muscles, particularly in the neck, shoulders, and jaw, may become tight and strained.
    - This can lead to discomfort and physical stiffness during social encounters.

These physical responses are beneficial in genuine danger but can exacerbate anxiety in social situations, making individuals feel more uncomfortable and anxious.

Techniques for Managing Physical Symptoms

1. **Grounding Techniques**
    - **Breath Focus**: Concentrate on slow, deep breaths to calm the nervous system. Breathing deeply into the diaphragm helps counteract the rapid, shallow breathing associated with anxiety.
    - **Sensory Engagement**: Engage in activities that involve the senses. For example, focus on the texture of an object in your hand or listen to soothing sounds. This helps divert attention from anxiety and anchors you in the present.

2. **Mindfulness Practices**
    - **Present-Moment Awareness**: Stay fully engaged in the current moment, observing thoughts and feelings without

judgment. Recognize that anxiety is a temporary state, not a permanent condition.

- **Self-Awareness**: Acknowledge physical symptoms, such as a racing heart, as manifestations of anxiety. Remind yourself that these symptoms are not indicative of imminent danger but are simply part of the anxiety experience.

3. **Cognitive Distortions**

    - **Identifying Irrational Thoughts**: Common cognitive distortions include catastrophizing (expecting the worst possible outcome) and mind-reading (assuming others are judging you negatively). Identifying these patterns is crucial for effective management.

    - **Reframing Thoughts**: Challenge and reframe distorted thoughts into more balanced perspectives. For instance, replace *Everyone will think I'm foolish if I make a mistake* with *Mistakes are a normal part of learning, and everyone makes them.*

4. **Controlled Breathing**

    - **Diaphragmatic Breathing**: Focus on deep breaths that engage the diaphragm. Inhale slowly through the nose, allowing the belly to rise, and then exhale gently through the mouth. This technique promotes relaxation and reduces stress.

    - **Box Breathing**: Follow a structured pattern of inhaling for four seconds, holding the breath for four seconds, exhaling for four seconds, and pausing for another four seconds. This method helps regulate breathing and calms the nervous system.

5. **Grounding Practices**: This exercise shifts focus from anxious thoughts to sensory experiences, grounding you in the present moment and reducing stress.

- **5-4-3-2-1 Exercise**:
  - **Five Things You Can See**: Notice and name five objects around you.
  - **Four Things You Can Touch**: Focus on textures and sensations you can feel.
  - **Three Things You Can Hear**: Listen to ambient sounds in your environment.
  - **Two Things You Can Smell**: Identify and recognize different scents.
  - **One Thing You Can Taste**: Pay attention to the taste in your mouth or eat something to engage your taste buds.

Combining Techniques for Greater Effectiveness

Integrating these techniques can create a synergistic effect that significantly alleviates the physiological symptoms of social anxiety. For example:

- **Mindfulness and Controlled Breathing**: Combining mindfulness with controlled breathing enhances the effectiveness of both methods. While controlled breathing calms the body's stress response, mindfulness helps in reframing the mind's interpretation of anxiety-provoking situations.

Long-Term Benefits

Incorporating these strategies into daily routines can provide long-term benefits for individuals struggling with social anxiety:

- **Improved Stress Management**: Regular practice of grounding techniques, mindfulness, and controlled breathing strengthens the body's ability to manage stress and reduces the frequency and intensity of anxiety episodes.

- **Enhanced Social Interactions**: For adults with social anxiety, these methods can lead to improved social interactions and overall quality of life.

- **Therapeutic Applications**: Mental health professionals can use these techniques in therapeutic settings, providing clients with practical tools to effectively navigate and manage social anxiety.

Consistently using these strategies helps individuals manage their anxiety symptoms more effectively, resulting in a more rewarding and less stressful social experience.

Genetic Predispositions

Genetics play a critical role in understanding social anxiety. Twin studies have been instrumental in revealing that anxiety disorders, including social anxiety, have a heritable component. These studies demonstrate that if one twin suffers from an anxiety disorder, the likelihood of the other twin developing a similar condition is significantly higher than in non-twin siblings. This hereditary factor underscores the importance of examining one's genetic background when addressing social anxiety.

The identification of specific genes linked to neurotransmitter functions has further enriched our understanding. For example, variations in genes that influence serotonin and dopamine pathways can heighten susceptibility to anxiety disorders. Framing social anxiety as a biological issue rooted in genetics helps to reduce the stigma associated with it. Recognizing the genetic underpinnings shifts the narrative from blaming individuals for their anxiety to appreciating the complex interplay of biology and the environment.

Moreover, insights gained from genetic research have profound implications for treatment. Knowledge of an individual's genetic makeup enables more personalized therapeutic plans. Traditional treatments like cognitive-behavioral therapy or medication might be optimized by considering genetic factors, potentially enhancing their effectiveness. Personalized treatment plans that take into account genetic predispositions could result in more successful anxiety management strategies.

Advances in genetic testing offer exciting prospects for future therapies. As genetic profiling becomes more sophisticated, it may become possible to develop tailored treatments based on an individual's unique genetic blueprint. For instance, certain genetic profiles may respond better to specific types of medication or therapeutic interventions, thereby improving outcomes for those struggling with social anxiety. Customizing treatment enhances its effectiveness and reduces the trial-and-error approach often used in managing anxiety disorders.

The promise of genetic testing extends beyond just treatment. It holds the potential to identify at-risk individuals before symptoms even manifest, allowing for early interventions that could mitigate the severity of social anxiety later in life. Early identification and intervention are keys to managing social anxiety more effectively and reducing its long-term impact on individuals.

Influence of Past Experiences and Trauma

Early childhood experiences play a crucial role in shaping social behavior and, consequently, the development of social anxiety. From birth, the interactions children have with their caregivers form the foundation for their future social interactions. Positive experiences can foster a sense of security and confidence, while negative or inconsistent interactions may lead to feelings of insecurity and heightened anxiety.

Traumatic events during childhood can have lasting impacts on an individual's mental health. Children who experience trauma often develop a hyper-awareness of perceived threats in their environment. This vigilance can extend into adulthood, manifesting as heightened anxiety in social situations. For instance, a child who has experienced bullying may grow up to be more cautious and anxious in social settings, always anticipating negative judgment or rejection. This hyper-awareness necessitates trauma-informed care, where mental health professionals recognize the profound impact trauma has on an individual's behavior and anxiety levels.

Experiences of social rejection also significantly affect self-esteem and social anxiety. When individuals face rejection from peers, especially during formative years, it can damage their self-image and lead to feelings of worthlessness. Such experiences teach them to anticipate rejection in future social interactions, exacerbating their anxiety. Adults who faced frequent rejection in school might avoid social gatherings, fearing similar outcomes. Strategies to navigate these feelings include cognitive-behavioral techniques that help reframe negative thoughts and build self-confidence.

A powerful method for mitigating the effects of traumatic memories is through transforming and retelling one's narrative. Revisiting painful experiences with the intent to reshape the story can provide immense healing. Narrative therapy, for example, encourages individuals to externalize their problems and examine them from various perspectives. This approach can diminish the control these memories have over them. Transforming a narrative from one of victimhood to resilience can empower individuals and decrease their social anxiety over time.

Understanding the impact of early childhood experiences, trauma, and social rejection is essential for both individuals dealing with social anxiety and the professionals supporting them. Recognizing these underlying factors allows for more empathetic and effective approaches to treatment. It underscores the importance of creating supportive environments for children and offering trauma-informed care for those impacted by adverse experiences.

Childhood experiences are not just fleeting moments but foundational elements that shape one's social behavior and mental health trajectory. These early interactions, whether nurturing or neglectful, lay the groundwork for how individuals perceive themselves and others. Positive reinforcement and secure attachments foster healthy social skills, while neglect or abuse can lead to anxiety and distrust. Parents, educators, and caregivers play pivotal roles in ensuring that children develop strong, positive social connections.

Trauma's role in developing social anxiety cannot be overstated. Traumatic experiences, particularly during vulnerable developmental stages, create long-lasting scars. The brain's response to trauma often results in a heightened state of alertness, making social interactions daunting. Trauma survivors frequently perceive neutral or benign social cues as threatening, leading to avoidance behaviors. This heightened state of arousal requires specialized therapeutic interventions that address both the psychological and physiological aspects of trauma.

Social rejection, especially during adolescence, can lead to profound self-doubt and anxiety. Adolescence is a period where peer acceptance is paramount, and rejection can leave deep emotional wounds. These experiences teach individuals to expect negative evaluations from others, promoting a cycle of avoidance and isolation. Addressing these fears involves rebuilding self-esteem and teaching coping mechanisms to handle social interactions more confidently. Social skills training and group therapy can provide safe spaces for individuals to practice and improve their social interactions.

Healing from traumatic experiences involves more than just coping mechanisms; it demands a re-examination and reshaping of one's story. Narrative therapy offers a way to reinterpret past events, turning traumatic memories into stories of strength and survival rather than victimhood. Changing the narrative allows individuals to reclaim their power and lessen the influence that negative memories have on their social interactions. This therapeutic process emphasizes the human capacity for resilience and growth, highlighting the potential for positive change even after significant adversity.

In essence, understanding the historical context of an individual's social anxiety provides a comprehensive view of their current struggles. Early experiences, trauma, and social rejection are intertwined factors that contribute to the development and persistence of social anxiety. Mental health professionals must consider these elements when designing treatment plans, ensuring that interventions are holistic and tailored to the individual's unique history.

Effective treatment for social anxiety involves recognizing and addressing the deep-seated roots of the condition. It's not just about managing symptoms but understanding the origins and triggers of anxiety. For many, this journey begins with exploring their past and uncovering the events that shaped their social behavior. Through this exploration, individuals can gain insights into their anxiety, paving the way for more targeted and effective interventions.

The role of caregivers and supportive figures cannot be underestimated. Their influence during critical developmental periods can either mitigate or exacerbate the effects of adverse experiences. Providing children with stable, nurturing environments can buffer against the development of social anxiety, while inconsistent or harmful interactions can set the stage for future struggles. Educating caregivers about the importance of their role and equipping them with tools to support healthy social development is crucial.

Traumatic experiences require sensitive and specialized care. Traditional therapeutic approaches may not suffice for individuals with deep-seated trauma. Instead, trauma-informed care focuses on creating a safe and supportive therapeutic environment where individuals feel understood and validated. Techniques such as EMDR (Eye Movement Desensitization and Reprocessing) and somatic therapies address the physical manifestations of trauma, helping individuals find relief from their anxiety.

Social rejection's impact on self-esteem highlights the need for interventions that rebuild confidence and promote positive self-assessment. Cognitive-behavioral strategies can help individuals challenge negative beliefs about themselves and develop healthier, more balanced self-perceptions. Additionally, fostering environments that encourage acceptance and inclusivity can reduce the prevalence of social rejection and its associated anxiety.

Transforming and retelling one's narrative offers hope and empowerment. It allows individuals to take control of their story, shifting from a passive recipient of events to an active agent of change. This process facilitates healing and promotes a sense of agency and resilience. Reframing their experiences helps individuals reduce the impact of past traumas and cultivate a more positive, hopeful outlook on their social interactions.

This chapter has explored the psychological and physiological mechanisms underlying social anxiety, highlighting the important role of neurotransmitters like serotonin, dopamine, and norepinephrine. These chemical messengers regulate mood, emotions, and stress responses, and imbalances can intensify feelings of anxiety in social situations. The fight-or-flight response exacerbates social interactions by causing physical symptoms such as an increased heart rate and sweating, which heighten anxiety. To manage these physiological reactions, the chapter discusses grounding techniques, mindfulness practices, and controlled breathing as effective strategies.

Genetic predispositions and previous experiences, such as trauma and social rejection, play a significant role in the development and persistence of social anxiety. Understanding these factors enables individuals and mental health professionals to create more personalized and empathetic treatment plans. Tailored therapies that consider genetic information hold promise for more effective and precise interventions. Acknowledging that social anxiety arises from a mix of biological, psychological, and environmental factors highlights the need for a comprehensive approach to treatment and support.

CHAPTER 3
Identifying Your Triggers

Identifying triggers is a crucial step in managing social anxiety. Recognizing the specific situations that heighten feelings of discomfort or fear enables individuals to better prepare and apply coping strategies. Without this awareness, navigating social interactions with confidence becomes difficult. This chapter explores various contexts where social anxiety frequently occurs, offering readers the insights needed to identify their personal triggers.

In this chapter, we delve into common scenarios that frequently trigger social anxiety, such as large gatherings, public speaking, impromptu interactions, and encounters with authority figures. Each section explores the reasons these situations provoke anxiety and offers strategies for managing them effectively. We also consider the role of environmental settings and networking events in exacerbating social anxiety, providing practical tips for gradual exposure and preparation. Reflecting on past experiences and understanding personal triggers will equip readers to handle social situations with greater ease and confidence.

Types of Social Situations That Trigger Anxiety

Understanding the different contexts in which social anxiety often arises is crucial for identifying your specific triggers. Identifying these triggers allows you to better prepare for and handle situations that usually cause discomfort. Social anxiety manifests in various settings and scenarios. Let's explore some common contexts where this type of anxiety frequently appears.

One of the most common social scenarios that induce anxiety is large gatherings or parties. Many people with social anxiety find themselves feeling overwhelmed by the sheer number of people, the noise levels, and the informal nature of interactions. Recognizing that events like parties often heighten anxiety can provide a sense of comfort, helping individuals understand that their feelings are not unique and can be managed. For instance, you might notice that you start feeling anxious at the mere thought of attending a party. Knowing this is a trigger allows you to take steps to prepare mentally, such as practicing relaxation techniques beforehand or setting small, manageable goals for the event, like speaking to two new people.

Public speaking is another notorious trigger for social anxiety. The fear of being judged or making mistakes in front of an audience can be paralyzing. This fear isn't unfounded; public speaking puts you in a vulnerable position where all eyes are on you, making any perceived flaw feel magnified. However, recognizing this fear can also be empowering. Recognizing that public speaking is a common source of anxiety enables you to find targeted strategies to manage it, such as joining a public speaking group or practicing in smaller, less daunting environments. These experiences can help build confidence over time.

Spontaneous social interactions, such as unexpected conversations in the grocery store or bumping into an acquaintance, can be particularly stressful because of their unpredictability. Unlike planned social events, spontaneous interactions don't allow time for mental preparation, leading to heightened anxiety levels. Reflecting on past experiences where spontaneous interactions caused anxiety can promote greater self-awareness. Think about a time when you unexpectedly ran into someone you hadn't seen in years. What were your immediate reactions? How did your body respond? Understanding how unpredictability affects you physically and emotionally can help you develop ways to stay calm, such as grounding techniques or having a few conversation starters ready to ease the pressure.

Interactions with authority figures, such as bosses, teachers, or even respected colleagues, can also trigger significant anxiety. These interactions often bring about feelings of inadequacy or fear of judgment, as the power dynamics make you feel more vulnerable. For example, asking your boss for a raise or presenting a project to a senior manager can be daunting. It's important to recognize these feelings and understand that they are a common response to hierarchical dynamics. Anticipating these interactions and preparing responses or discussion points in advance allows you to approach them with greater calmness and confidence. Practicing mindfulness or seeking feedback from trusted peers can also alleviate some of this anxiety, enabling you to handle interactions with authority figures more effectively.

Certain environmental settings, such as cafes, networking events, or crowded public places, can carry emotional weight and trigger anxiety. These environments might be associated with past negative experiences or overwhelming stimuli that make you feel exposed. For instance, if you've had a panic attack in a crowded café before, merely walking past one might evoke anxiety. To prepare for these settings, try gradual exposure techniques. Start by spending short periods in these environments and slowly increase your time there as your comfort level grows. Bringing along a friend or engaging in a calming activity, like listening to music or reading, can also provide a sense of security and reduce anxiety.

Networking events deserve special mention due to their unique combination of formal and informal social expectations. The need to make a positive impression while engaging in meaningful conversations with strangers can create a high-pressure situation. If you've ever attended a networking event, you might recall the tension of introducing yourself, keeping the conversation flowing, and exchanging contact information—all while trying to appear confident and collected. Acknowledging these challenges helps in setting realistic expectations for yourself. Rather than aiming to speak to everyone in the room, focus on having a few quality conversations. Preparing a brief introduction about yourself and some key talking points related to your field can make these interactions smoother and less anxiety-inducing.

Reflecting on these different contexts and how they affect you is an essential step toward managing social anxiety. Each individual has unique triggers, and what causes anxiety for one person might not be an issue for another. Taking the time to identify and understand your specific triggers will enable you to adopt personalized coping strategies.

Personal Reflection Exercises

Reflecting on our experiences can offer invaluable insights into the hidden triggers of social anxiety. Examining these moments helps us identify the specific thoughts and feelings that emerge during anxious episodes, providing a strong foundation for effective management. One powerful tool in this self-reflective journey is journaling.

Journaling prompts serve as a guiding hand, leading us to explore our internal landscapes. For instance, you might start by writing about a recent social event that triggered anxiety: "Describe the last time you felt socially anxious. What was happening around you? What were you thinking and feeling?" This kind of targeted prompt helps to break down the experience into manageable parts, making it easier to identify underlying issues. Reflecting on questions like, "What were your physical sensations at that moment?" or "Did any particular thought keep recurring?" can reveal patterns that might otherwise go unnoticed. This method aids in recognizing triggers and fosters a habit of introspection, which can be beneficial for long-term mental health.

In tandem with journaling, self-assessment tools, and questionnaires can provide a structured approach to understanding personal strengths and weaknesses. Unlike open journaling, these tools often come with pre-defined questions that can spotlight areas needing more attention. For example, a questionnaire might ask you to rate your level of anxiety in different social settings, such as speaking in a meeting versus chatting with friends. These ratings help create a clearer picture of which situations are most challenging for you. Self-assessment tools can cover various facets of your personality and emotional responses, offering a comprehensive view of your social anxiety landscape. Over time, reviewing these assessments can show progress or highlight persistent issues, guiding further steps in your coping strategies.

Visualization techniques offer a practical method for addressing social anxiety. This approach involves mentally rehearsing anxiety-inducing scenarios in a controlled environment. Preparing in this way helps reduce surprises and build confidence for real-life situations. For example, if you feel anxious about a networking event, you might visualize yourself entering the room, greeting others, and engaging in conversations. Focus on every detail—the décor, the sounds, and even the texture of your clothes. Imagine yourself moving through the event with ease and handling any anxious moments gracefully. This mental rehearsal can make the actual experience less daunting and increase your emotional resilience.

After social interactions, taking time for post-engagement reviews can significantly enhance self-awareness. This practice involves reflecting on your feelings and behaviors immediately after a social event. Consider questions like, "How did I feel during the interaction?" or "Were there moments when my anxiety was particularly high or low?" Analyzing these reflections can shed light on specific triggers and help you understand what worked well and what didn't. For example, you might notice that you felt more relaxed when you had a supportive friend nearby or that small talk is more manageable than deep conversations. These insights can inform future strategies, making each social engagement a learning opportunity.

Collectively, these reflective practices—journaling prompts, self-assessment tools, visualization techniques, and post-social engagement reviews—create a robust framework for identifying and understanding the triggers of social anxiety. They bring clarity to the sources of anxiety and pave the way for developing personalized coping mechanisms. Consistently applying these methods can help readers shift from feeling helpless about social anxiety to actively managing it.

As you delve into these exercises, it's crucial to approach them with patience and compassion. The process of uncovering and confronting your triggers can be emotionally taxing, and it's okay to take breaks when needed. Each step, no matter how small, is a progress toward greater self-awareness and control over your social anxiety. Over time, these practices will contribute to a deeper understanding of yourself and more effective strategies for navigating social interactions.

Engaging with these tools regularly can also make them more potent. Just as physical exercise strengthens muscles over time, mental exercises like journaling and visualization fortify your emotional resilience. The consistency of exploring your thoughts, emotions, and reactions helps solidify new, healthier patterns of thinking and behaving. Moreover, documenting your journey provides a tangible record of growth, which can be incredibly empowering.

For those seeking additional support, sharing your insights with a therapist or counselor can add another layer of benefit. Mental health professionals can offer guidance tailored to your unique experiences, helping you interpret your reflections and develop targeted strategies. They can also introduce you to other therapeutic techniques that complement your self-reflection practices, creating a holistic approach to managing social anxiety.

Documenting Anxious Moments

One of the most empowering tools in managing social anxiety is the consistent documentation of anxious moments through daily anxiety logs. While this may seem like a simple exercise, it carries profound implications for those seeking to understand their anxiety better and implement effective coping strategies. Recording each instance of heightened anxiety allows individuals to objectively analyze their patterns over time.

Daily anxiety logs serve as a mirror reflecting the frequency and intensity of one's anxieties. This method encourages accountability and allows for a clearer understanding of how often these moments occur and under what circumstances. For example, if you notice that your anxiety spikes before attending meetings at work or social gatherings, this insight can drive more tailored coping mechanisms. It's about creating a factual record that doesn't rely on memory alone, which can sometimes be clouded by the emotional weight of the experience.

Furthermore, regular review of these logs plays a pivotal role in highlighting recurring themes. These patterns can reveal specific triggers—like certain environments, social situations, or even particular times of day—that consistently provoke anxiety. Recognizing these themes enables you to anticipate anxiety-provoking situations and prepare accordingly. For instance, if you identify public speaking as a common trigger, preparing for presentations with extra practice and relaxation techniques can reduce the anticipated anxiety.

Sharing these logs with trusted friends or mental health professionals can introduce new perspectives and strategies. Often, others can see patterns or offer advice that might not be immediately obvious to you. This collaborative sharing transforms the personal battle with anxiety into a community effort, enhancing support networks and fostering a sense of solidarity. A friend might suggest practicing deep-breathing exercises they've found helpful, while a therapist could provide professional techniques like cognitive-behavioral strategies tailored to your specific triggers.

Setting small, achievable goals based on insights from your anxiety logs supports gradual exposure to challenging situations. For example, if social interactions cause anxiety, begin with simple tasks like greeting a coworker or asking a question in a meeting. Gradually increase the difficulty of these interactions as your confidence grows. This approach, known as exposure therapy, helps reduce anxiety by systematically addressing feared scenarios in a controlled way. Tackle this process with patience and kindness toward yourself. Progress may be gradual, and setbacks are a normal part of the journey. Persistence and ongoing reflection are essential for navigating social anxiety with greater resilience and insight.

Pattern Recognition and Common Themes

Identifying patterns in social anxiety is a crucial step toward managing and overcoming it. Recognizing these patterns allows individuals to start addressing the underlying issues that contribute to their anxiety. One effective method to achieve this is by analyzing logs for themes. Keeping a record of anxiety-inducing situations allows one to review and identify recurring themes and triggers. This analysis promotes deeper self-insight, revealing the underlying causes behind specific anxieties. For example, if an individual frequently notes feeling anxious in large groups, this could indicate a broader issue with social settings or feeling overwhelmed by too many stimuli.

Identifying emotional triggers associated with anxiety is crucial for effective management. Emotional triggers are particular feelings or emotions that provoke anxiety responses. Recognizing these triggers allows individuals to develop more effective strategies for managing their anxiety. For example, if someone discovers that feelings of inadequacy trigger their social anxiety, they can focus on building self-confidence and addressing negative self-perceptions. Techniques like cognitive reframing, which involves challenging and replacing negative thoughts with more positive ones, can be especially beneficial in managing these emotional triggers.

Developing action plans provides structured approaches for confronting anxiety-inducing situations systematically. An action plan acts as a roadmap, outlining steps to take when facing anxiety-provoking scenarios. This might include gradual exposure to feared situations, starting with less intimidating environments and slowly working up to more challenging ones. For example, if public speaking induces anxiety, an action plan could involve initially speaking in front of a small, familiar group before progressing to larger and less familiar audiences. Structured action plans provide a clear path and help reduce the overwhelming nature of facing anxiety head-on.

Engaging in discussions with peers creates valuable opportunities for learning new strategies and reinforces shared experiences. Talking about anxiety with others who understand can offer fresh perspectives and coping mechanisms that one might not have considered. Additionally, it cultivates a sense of community and support, reassuring individuals that they are not alone in their experiences. Peer discussion groups or therapy sessions can be excellent platforms for sharing and learning. For instance, hearing how a peer successfully managed a similar anxiety-inducing situation can inspire and motivate others to try new approaches themselves.

Analyzing logs for themes should include setting aside regular time for reflection. Reviewing logs weekly can help identify patterns that might not be immediately apparent. Over time, these reviews will highlight persistent themes, whether they are related to specific people, places, or types of events. Once these patterns are identified, individuals can begin to anticipate and prepare for situations that trigger their anxiety. This anticipation allows for proactive measures, such as practicing relaxation techniques or having a prepared response strategy.

Emotional triggers often come hand-in-hand with physical symptoms. Recognizing both emotional and physical signs of anxiety can provide a comprehensive understanding of one's reactions. Physical symptoms like sweating, rapid heartbeat, and trembling can serve as indicators that an emotional trigger has been activated. Being aware of these physical cues allows individuals to intervene early and use anxiety-reducing techniques like deep breathing or mindfulness exercises. For instance, recognizing the onset of sweaty palms during a conversation can trigger a prompt mental check-in and the application of calming methods.

When developing action plans, it is beneficial to personalize them according to individual needs and preferences. There is no one-size-fits-all approach to managing anxiety, so customizing action plans ensures they are practical and relevant. Individuals should consider what environments make them feel most comfortable and what types of support they may need. For instance, someone might find it helpful to bring a friend along to a social event for additional support. Others might prefer practicing relaxation techniques right before the engaging scenario. Tailoring action plans in this way enhances their effectiveness and ensures they are more likely to be followed.

Peer discussions can also introduce individuals to various tools and resources that they might not have discovered on their own. For example, someone might recommend a helpful book on anxiety management or share information about a useful mobile app designed for mental health tracking. These recommendations can expand an individual's toolkit for managing anxiety, providing additional layers of support. Additionally, the feedback and encouragement from peers can reinforce the progress made, building confidence and motivation to continue working toward overcoming social anxiety.

In this chapter, we examined different social situations that frequently trigger anxiety and discussed how identifying these scenarios can help you prepare more effectively. Whether it's large gatherings, public speaking, impromptu interactions, or encounters with authority figures, each situation presents its own set of challenges. Recognizing these triggers is crucial for creating personalized strategies to handle them with greater confidence. Reflecting on past experiences in these contexts provides valuable insights into your emotional reactions, enabling you to implement proactive management techniques such as gradual exposure and mindfulness practices.

Identifying your specific triggers and using tools like journaling and self-assessment can better prepare you to handle anxiety-provoking situations. Visualization and post-event reviews further strengthen your ability to anticipate and manage anxious moments, promoting greater self-awareness. Keeping regular records of anxious episodes helps identify patterns and recurring themes while sharing these records with trusted individuals can offer fresh perspectives and support. Consistently applying these methods can transform your approach to social anxiety, shifting from a reactive stance to proactive and mindful management, and ultimately enhancing your social interactions and overall quality of life.

CHAPTER 4
Cognitive-Behavioral Techniques

Cognitive-behavioral techniques are valuable tools for managing social anxiety. These methods help individuals recognize and shift negative thought patterns, fostering a healthier mental outlook and improving their reactions in social situations. Focusing on the roots of anxiety, cognitive-behavioral techniques empower individuals to gain control over their thoughts and behaviors, ultimately improving their social interactions and enhancing their quality of life.

This chapter explores a range of strategies aimed at addressing social anxiety. We begin by focusing on identifying and challenging negative thoughts through practical exercises like thought records. We'll then delve into reframing techniques to help transform negative perspectives into positive or realistic viewpoints. Additionally, we will discuss the creation and use of positive affirmations to counteract negative self-talk. Our goal is to equip readers with a comprehensive understanding of cognitive-behavioral techniques that foster resilience and enhance coping mechanisms in social situations.

Challenging Negative Thoughts

Identifying and challenging negative thought patterns is a crucial aspect of managing social anxiety. Recognizing cognitive distortions is the first step on the journey toward developing healthier thinking habits. Cognitive distortions are irrational thought patterns that influence one's perception of reality. Two common distortions contributing to social anxiety are overgeneralization and catastrophizing.

Overgeneralization involves making broad statements based on a single event. Someone might think, *I always mess up in social situations*, after one awkward encounter. This type of thinking can trap individuals in a cycle of negativity, affecting their self-esteem and confidence. Catastrophizing, on the other hand, involves expecting the worst possible outcome in any situation. For instance, if someone stumbles over their words during a presentation, they might fear that everyone now thinks less of them. Recognizing these distortions is the first step in addressing them.

Thought records are practical tools to capture and evaluate negative thoughts systematically. They provide a structured format to identify triggers, emotional responses, and the accompanying thoughts. Through this process, individuals can gain insight into their automatic thoughts and how these contribute to their anxiety. A typical thought record includes columns for the situation, emotions experienced, automatic thoughts, evidence supporting the thought, evidence against it, and a more balanced thought. This method encourages a critical examination of negative thoughts and reinforces the habit of looking at situations more objectively.

Consistently using thought records helps cultivate a mindset of questioning and evaluating negative thoughts rather than accepting them as facts. Over time, this practice can lead to significant changes in how individuals perceive social situations and manage their anxiety.

Reframing techniques are another powerful strategy for transforming negative thoughts into positive or realistic scenarios. Reframing involves shifting the perspective from which one views a situation. Instead of seeing a social interaction as a potential failure, one can reframe it as an opportunity to learn and grow. For instance, if someone feels anxious about attending a social event due to fears of being judged, they can reframe this thought by reminding themselves that most people are typically more focused on their own experiences than on evaluating others.

Reframing reduces anxiety and opens up possibilities for positive outcomes. It promotes a more balanced perspective, recognizing both strengths and opportunities for growth. Consistently practicing reframing allows individuals to build resilience and approach social situations with a more constructive mindset.

Creating and using positive affirmations is another valuable technique to combat negative self-talk. Affirmations are positive statements that help reinforce a sense of self-worth and counteract negative beliefs. For individuals experiencing social anxiety, affirmations can serve as reminders of their abilities and potential. For instance, repeating statements like *I am confident in social situations* or *I handle social interactions with ease* can help shift the focus from negative thoughts to empowering ones.

The effectiveness of affirmations lies in their ability to reshape one's internal dialogue. When repeated consistently, they can gradually alter deep-seated beliefs and foster a more positive self-image. It's crucial to select affirmations that personally resonate and feel genuine. Writing them down and reciting them daily can make them more ingrained in one's thought patterns.

In addition to these techniques, it's essential to approach the process of challenging negative thoughts with patience and self-compassion. Changing long-standing thought patterns takes time and effort. It's normal to have setbacks along the way, but each step forward contributes to overall progress. Celebrating small victories and acknowledging growth can reinforce motivation and commitment to the journey.

Exposure Therapy Basics

Exposure therapy is an evidence-based cognitive-behavioral technique designed to help individuals face their fears and reduce anxiety, particularly in social situations. At its core, exposure therapy encourages confronting rather than avoiding feared situations, which can gradually diminish the power these fears hold over an individual.

Understanding exposure therapy begins with recognizing that avoidance often exacerbates anxiety. When a person avoids social situations due to fear, it may provide immediate relief but ultimately reinforces the anxiety. Repeatedly facing feared scenarios through exposure therapy helps individuals learn that the anticipated negative outcomes are unlikely or manageable, thus diminishing their anxiety over time.

A critical component of exposure therapy is developing a hierarchy of feared situations. This list arranges scenarios from the least to most anxiety-provoking. For example, a person with social anxiety might place speaking in front of a trusted friend at the lower end of their fear scale, while giving a public speech to a large audience ranks at the highest level. Establishing this hierarchy provides a structured and gradual approach to facing their fears.

To develop an effective hierarchy, one must begin by identifying specific situations that trigger anxiety. It's helpful to break these down into detailed steps. Instead of listing "attending a party," one might include "entering the party," "greeting acquaintances," and "joining a conversation." This nuanced breakdown provides clear targets for each exposure session, making the process more manageable.

Once the hierarchy is established, the next step involves starting with lower-level fears. Initially, the individual engages in scenarios that cause mild anxiety. Success in these situations builds confidence and resilience. For instance, if the least provoking scenario is greeting a neighbor, the individual might practice this repeatedly until it no longer induces significant stress.

Gradual desensitization is the essence of this process. As comfort with lower-level fears increases, the individual incrementally progresses to more challenging situations outlined in their hierarchy. Each step should be approached methodically, ensuring sufficient practice and reflection before advancing. Jumping too quickly to high-anxiety situations can be counterproductive, potentially reinforcing fear if the experience is overwhelmingly stressful.

Reflection after each exposure session is vital. This involves considering what happened, how one felt, and what was learned. Keeping a journal can be beneficial for tracking progress and identifying patterns in responses. Reflecting helps uncover insights about personal reactions and outcomes, which can inform future strategies and adjustments.

Reflecting on experiences often reveals that feared outcomes rarely occur as expected. For instance, during a small talk, you might find that the conversation flowed more smoothly than anticipated and that others responded positively. Acknowledging these positive outcomes strengthens resilience and diminishes the belief that social interactions are inherently threatening.

Additionally, reflecting on these experiences can highlight areas needing further development. If certain situations continue to provoke high anxiety, it may be helpful to introduce additional intermediate steps. For example, if speaking in a meeting remains intimidating despite successes in smaller groups, you might first try leading a discussion with a few colleagues to ease the transition.

The support of a therapist or counselor can enhance the effectiveness of exposure therapy. These professionals can help structure the hierarchy, provide encouragement, and offer coping strategies for particularly challenging exposures. They also assist in fostering a safe and supportive environment for individuals to confront their fears.

Decatastrophizing Techniques

Minimizing catastrophic thinking is a crucial element in managing social anxiety. This approach involves examining and reframing the exaggerated, fearful thoughts that often drive social anxiety. One effective technique to address this is reality testing. Individuals should start by identifying the worst-case scenarios they fear and then questioning the likelihood of these events occurring.

Let's consider a common situation: giving a presentation at work. Someone might think, *I'll forget my lines, everyone will laugh at me, and I'll get fired.* Using reality testing, you can break down these fears. How likely is it that you'll forget every line? Even if you miss some points, will your colleagues actually laugh at you? Is getting fired a realistic consequence for a less-than-perfect presentation? Often, when you analyze these catastrophic thoughts, you find that the worst-case scenario is unlikely.

Furthermore, engaging in a cost-benefit analysis of anxiety-driven thoughts and behaviors can provide significant insights. This involves weighing the pros and cons of holding onto these negative beliefs and the subsequent actions based on them. Returning to the presentation example, what are the costs of believing you'll fail? Increased stress, sleepless nights, and perhaps avoiding future speaking opportunities altogether. On the flip side, what benefits might come from challenging these thoughts? Reduced anxiety, improved performance, and greater confidence in public speaking.

Conducting a cost-benefit analysis requires honest self-reflection. Ask yourself whether the energy spent worrying about unlikely outcomes could be put to better use. Often, individuals find that their anxiety offers little benefit while contributing heavily to their distress. Recognizing this imbalance can motivate them to adopt healthier perspectives.

Another useful technique is visualizing possible outcomes in a more positive light using imagery techniques. Visualization involves mentally creating detailed and vivid images of oneself successfully navigating feared situations. Before the presentation, imagine yourself speaking confidently, delivering your points clearly, and receiving appreciative nods from your audience. Regularly visualizing positive outcomes helps train your brain to expect success instead of failure.

Imagery techniques serve as mental rehearsals. Just as athletes visualize peak performance before a game, individuals with social anxiety can use this strategy to prepare for social interactions. Over time, these positive visualizations can replace the default mental imagery of failure and embarrassment, fostering a sense of readiness and calmness.

Developing self-affirming and constructive internal dialogue through positive self-talk is another powerful method. Positive self-talk involves replacing self-critical thoughts with encouraging and empowering statements. Instead of thinking, *I always mess up*, you can tell yourself, *I have prepared well, and I can do this*. Such affirmations may seem simple, but they can significantly shift your emotional response to social situations.

Implementing positive self-talk starts with awareness. Pay attention to your inner monologue, especially during moments of stress or anticipation. When you notice negative self-talk, consciously counter it with positive affirmations. Initially, this practice may feel forced or unnatural, but consistency is key. Over time, these positive statements can become second nature, providing a reliable source of comfort and motivation.

Developing a Growth Mindset

Adopting a growth mindset is pivotal in managing social anxiety as it empowers individuals to embrace challenges and foster resilience. Understanding the distinction between a growth mindset and a fixed mindset is the first step. A growth mindset, as coined by psychologist Carol Dweck, implies that abilities and intelligence can be developed through dedication and hard work. This contrasts with a fixed mindset, wherein people believe their qualities are immutable traits. Recognizing these differences helps to illuminate how adopting a growth mindset can positively impact one's approach to social interactions.

Individuals with a growth mindset view challenges as opportunities for personal growth rather than threats to avoid. Embracing challenges functions as a stepping stone toward improvement, creating an environment conducive to learning and adaptation. Encouraging readers to confront social anxiety involves reframing their perception of challenges. Instead of seeing an overwhelming social situation as a potential failure, consider it a valuable experience that contributes to one's development. For instance, attending a social event where you feel anxious can be perceived not as an impending catastrophe but as a chance to practice and refine social skills.

Valuing constructive feedback is essential for nurturing a growth mindset. Social anxiety often arises from a fear of negative judgment, but viewing feedback as a tool for improvement can help alleviate this fear. Constructive criticism provides valuable insights into areas for growth and offers practical steps for enhancement. For instance, if a friend mentions that you occasionally seem disengaged during conversations, interpret this not as a personal attack but as a helpful observation. Use this feedback to refine your listening skills and enhance your communication methods. Adopting this perspective turns feedback from a potential source of anxiety into an opportunity for growth and development.

Recognizing and celebrating small wins is vital to maintaining motivation and tracking progress in managing social anxiety. Breaking down larger goals into manageable achievements makes the overall journey less daunting and more rewarding. Small victories, such as initiating a conversation or maintaining eye contact during a social interaction, should be acknowledged and celebrated. These successes, no matter how minor they may seem, represent significant strides toward overcoming social anxiety. Celebrating them reinforces positive behavior, making it easier to tackle bigger challenges over time.

To effectively embrace challenges as a means of personal growth, set clear and achievable goals. Begin with less intimidating social scenarios and gradually progress to more challenging ones. This methodical approach helps build confidence incrementally, reducing the intensity of anxiety associated with more daunting situations. For instance, start by practicing small talk with a colleague before attempting to engage in a group discussion at a social gathering. Each step forward, however minor, lays the foundation for overcoming larger fears.

Similarly, accepting constructive feedback requires a mindset shift. Cultivate an attitude that views feedback as an essential component of growth rather than a reflection of personal inadequacy. When receiving feedback, take a moment to reflect on its content objectively. Ask yourself what actionable insights can be derived and how they can be implemented to improve your social interactions. Maintaining a journal to document feedback and track improvements can be a useful strategy in this process. Over time, this practice helps to internalize the value of feedback as a constructive rather than destructive element.

In terms of celebrating progress, make it a habit to acknowledge and reward yourself for the efforts you've put in. Rewards do not have to be extravagant; simple acknowledgments or treats suffice. The key is to recognize the effort and courage required to face social anxiety head-on. Consider keeping a progress diary where you jot down each accomplishment, no matter how insignificant it may appear. Reviewing this diary regularly serves as a potent reminder of your journey and the progress made, bolstering your morale and determination.

This chapter has examined several cognitive-behavioral techniques aimed at managing social anxiety through the adjustment of negative thoughts and behaviors. By recognizing and challenging cognitive distortions—such as overgeneralization and catastrophizing—individuals can cultivate healthier thinking patterns. Tools like thought records and reframing provide structured approaches to evaluate and modify automatic thoughts, fostering more balanced viewpoints.

Furthermore, positive affirmations serve as a way to combat negative self-talk and gradually build a more positive self-image.

In addition, we explored the role of exposure therapy in gradually addressing feared situations to effectively lower anxiety levels. By creating a hierarchy of feared scenarios and tackling them step by step, individuals can build resilience and boost their confidence in social contexts. Reality testing and cost-benefit analysis offer structured methods to counteract catastrophic thinking. Visualization of positive outcomes and positive self-talk further aid in managing social anxiety. Embracing a growth mindset throughout this process is essential, as it fosters a focus on personal development and ongoing improvement.

CHAPTER 5
Mindfulness and Relaxation Strategies

Mindfulness and relaxation techniques are essential for managing social anxiety, equipping individuals with the tools to calm their minds and improve emotional well-being. These practices offer immediate stress relief and help build long-term resilience, fostering confidence in social situations. Incorporating methods like mindful breathing, guided meditation, and progressive muscle relaxation into daily routines can help individuals develop a sense of inner peace and emotional stability. These strategies are invaluable for anyone looking to navigate and thrive in social environments.

This chapter explores various mindfulness and relaxation techniques aimed at reducing social anxiety. It begins with a look at different breathing exercises, such as diaphragmatic breathing, the 4-7-8 technique, and square breathing, each offering distinct stress-reducing benefits. We then discuss guided meditation practices and how they enhance mindfulness through structured sessions and visualization techniques. Additionally, the chapter introduces loving-kindness meditation, which promotes compassion and empathy, further helping to alleviate social anxiety. Finally, it covers progressive muscle relaxation (PMR), detailing its step-by-step application and significant impact on physical and psychological health. With practical examples and detailed guidelines, this chapter provides readers with a comprehensive toolkit to effectively manage and overcome social anxiety.

Breathing Exercises

Breathing Techniques for Anxiety Reduction

Diaphragmatic Breathing

Diaphragmatic breathing, also known as abdominal or belly breathing, is a fundamental technique that focuses on deep breathing from the diaphragm. When we breathe deeply, our diaphragm contracts and moves downward, creating more space in the chest cavity and allowing the lungs to expand fully. This method of breathing activates the parasympathetic nervous system, which promotes a state of calmness and relaxation, essential for grounding the mind.

1. Settle into a comfortable sitting or lying position, ensuring your shoulders are relaxed.
2. Rest one hand on your chest and the other on your abdomen.
3. Take a deep breath in through your nose, allowing your abdomen to expand while keeping your chest relatively still.
4. Exhale slowly through your mouth, feeling your abdomen contract.

Engage in this practice for five to ten minutes daily, especially during moments of heightened anxiety, to develop a conscious awareness of your breath. Consistent practice can significantly improve your ability to manage stress and enhance overall well-being.

4-7-8 Breathing Technique

The 4-7-8 breathing technique, popularized by Dr. Andrew Weil, is an effective method for quickly managing acute anxiety. This breathing pattern involves inhaling for four seconds, holding the breath for seven seconds, and exhaling for eight seconds. This specific ratio helps slow down the heart rate and induces a state of profound relaxation.

Here's how to practice the 4-7-8 technique:

1. Sit or lie down comfortably, keeping the tip of your tongue against the ridge behind your upper front teeth throughout the exercise.
2. Exhale completely, emptying your lungs.
3. Inhale quietly through your nose for a count of four seconds.
4. Hold your breath for seven seconds.
5. Exhale strongly through your mouth, making a "whoosh" sound, for eight seconds.

Repeat this cycle up to four times initially, and as you become more comfortable, gradually increase the repetitions. It is advisable to practice this technique when you are seated or lying down to prevent dizziness, particularly if you experience lightheadedness during the first few attempts. According to Medical News Today, while clinical research on this technique is limited, many users report significant anxiety reduction and improved sleep quality after practicing consistently (Fletcher, 2019).

Square Breathing

Square breathing, also known as box breathing, is another powerful technique that pairs breathing with visualization. This method helps manage panic by providing a rhythmic focus, directing attention away from anxiety symptoms. Square breathing is simple enough for beginners and involves visualizing a square to regulate your breath.

Here's a step-by-step guide to practicing square breathing:

1. Sit comfortably with your feet flat on the ground and your back straight.
2. Picture a square in front of you.
3. Inhale through your nose for a count of four, imagining yourself tracing the first side of the square.
4. Hold your breath for a count of four, visualizing the second side of the square.
5. Exhale through your mouth for a count of four, envisioning the third side of the square.
6. Hold your breath again for a count of four, completing the final side of the square.

Repeat this sequence for several minutes. The act of visualizing a square provides a structured cadence that eases the mind and body into a more tranquil state. This technique can be particularly useful during high-stress situations or before engaging in social interactions that typically trigger anxiety.

Mindful Breathing Focus

Mindful breathing is about creating an awareness of your breath and bodily sensations. This practice encourages you to stay present in the moment, helping to build a buffer against overwhelming emotions. Mindful breathing doesn't require a strict pattern or timing, making it flexible and accessible even in the midst of anxiety.

To practice mindful breathing:

1. Choose a quiet, interruption-free space.
2. Sit or lie down in a comfortable position.
3. Close your eyes and take a few deep breaths to ease into the practice.
4. Observe the natural rhythm of your breath without attempting to alter it.

5. Pay attention to the sensations of air entering and leaving your nostrils, the rise and fall of your chest, or the expansion and contraction of your abdomen.

If your mind starts to wander, gently bring your focus back to your breath. The aim of mindful breathing is not necessarily to control the breath but to observe it and remain grounded in the present moment. This practice can cultivate a sense of inner peace, making it easier to navigate through stressful situations.

Integrating These Techniques

Incorporating these breathing techniques into your daily routine can provide substantial benefits in managing anxiety. Diaphragmatic breathing and 4-7-8 breathing may serve as foundational practices, while square breathing and mindful breathing can be utilized as supplementary tools tailored to specific needs and circumstances. Dedicating time to practice these techniques can help you develop greater resilience and equip you with practical strategies to maintain calmness in challenging social settings.

Guided Meditation Practices

In today's fast-paced world, guided meditation offers an accessible way to enhance mindfulness and reduce social anxiety. This subpoint explores guided meditation, providing insights into its practice and associated benefits.

Introduction to Guided Meditation

Guided meditation is a form of meditation led by a narrator or instructor who provides verbal guidance as you move through different phases of the meditation. It begins with establishing a comfortable position, followed by focusing on breathing and progressing to more intricate instructions like visualizing calming scenes or engaging in body scans. The intent is to lead the mind away from anxious thoughts, creating a space for relaxation and mental clarity. For those new to meditation, guided sessions offer structure and ease the daunting prospect of meditating in silence. Simultaneously, seasoned practitioners can deepen their practice by leveraging varied techniques introduced by different guides.

Meditation Apps and Resources

The digital age has made guided meditation more accessible through mobile apps and online resources. Platforms such as Headspace, Calm, and Insight Timer provide a wide array of guided meditations tailored to specific needs, including reducing social anxiety. Each app features sessions that vary in length and focus, making it easy to integrate these practices into daily routines, whether at home or on the go. Additionally, many of these apps offer specialized programs targeting stress relief, sleep improvement, emotional regulation, and more. These tools enable individuals to establish a consistent meditation practice that integrates seamlessly into their lifestyle.

Guideline: Choose a meditation app that aligns with your personal goals. Try different guided sessions to see which resonates best with you, and set aside time each day to engage with these resources.

Visualization Techniques

Visualization is a powerful component of guided meditation, using mental imagery to transform anxious thoughts into positive experiences. When practicing visualization, the guide may prompt you to imagine yourself in a serene environment, such as a tranquil beach or a lush forest. These images work by diverting attention from anxiety-provoking thoughts and fostering a sense of safety and calm. Another effective technique involves envisioning successful social interactions and reinforcing feelings of confidence and competence. Over time, regularly engaging in visualization can create new neural pathways that promote a more relaxed and optimistic mindset, thereby reducing instances of social anxiety.

Guideline: During your guided meditation, fully immerse yourself in the visualizations. Engage all your senses—imagine the sounds, smells, and textures of the scene. The more vivid your visualization, the more effective it will be in relieving anxiety.

Loving-Kindness Meditation

Loving-kindness meditation (LKM) is another valuable practice for addressing social anxiety. This form of meditation focuses on cultivating compassion and empathy toward oneself and others. Typically, LKM involves silently repeating phrases that convey goodwill, such as *May I be happy*, or *May you be safe*, while visualizing oneself or others. This practice can significantly shift one's mindset from self-criticism and fear toward warmth and acceptance. Research suggests that LKM can activate brain areas involved in emotional processing and empathy, promoting emotional resilience and interpersonal connection (Hofmann et al., 2011). For those struggling with social anxiety, fostering a compassionate attitude can be transformative, leading to more fulfilling and less stressful social interactions.

Guideline: Start your loving-kindness meditation by directing compassion toward yourself. Gradually extend these feelings toward friends, family, and eventually toward people you find challenging. This gradual expansion helps build genuine empathy and understanding.

Progressive Muscle Relaxation

Understanding PMR

Progressive Muscle Relaxation (PMR) is a technique designed to help individuals identify and manage physical tension, which is often linked to social anxiety. Developed by American physician Edmund Jacobson in the 1930s, PMR involves systematically tensing and then relaxing different muscle groups in the body. The main goal is to highlight the contrast between tension and relaxation, helping practitioners recognize muscle tightness and actively engage in releasing it.

For people with anxiety, muscular tension can become so habitual that it goes unnoticed. Through regular practice of PMR, individuals learn to discern the difference between a tense and relaxed muscle, making it easier to identify when their bodies are stressed. This heightened awareness serves as an early warning system, allowing for timely intervention before stress levels escalate. PMR also empowers individuals to cue relaxation responses whenever they start feeling anxious, providing a practical tool to combat physical symptoms of anxiety.

Step-by-Step PMR Guide

Practicing Progressive Muscle Relaxation requires a structured approach. Here's a step-by-step guide to get started:

1. **Find a Quiet Space**: Choose a calm environment where you won't be disturbed. Sit or lie down in a comfortable position, ensuring your clothing is loose and not restrictive. Close your eyes and take several slow, deep breaths to prepare yourself mentally and physically.

2. **Tension Phase**: Begin by focusing on one muscle group at a time, starting from either the top of your head or your feet. For example, if starting with your hands, clench your fist tightly. Hold this tension for about five seconds, making sure to feel the strain but stopping short if you experience pain or discomfort. It's important to isolate each muscle group to avoid tensing surrounding muscles.

3. **Relaxation Phase**: After holding the tension, quickly release the muscles and let go of all the tightness. Exhale deeply while doing so, and focus on the sensation of the muscle becoming loose and limp. Notice the stark difference between tension and relaxation; this awareness is crucial.

4. **Repeat for Other Muscle Groups**: Gradually work through other areas of your body, following the same process. Typical muscle groups include the forehead, jaw, shoulders,

arms, abdomen, and legs. Each session should last around 15-20 minutes to ensure thorough relaxation.

5. **Practice Regularly**: Initially, practice PMR twice daily until you become proficient. As you progress, you may find that shorter sessions are just as effective. Consistent practice will make it easier to induce relaxation quickly, especially when you sense anxiety coming on.

Integrating PMR Into Daily Life

Integrating PMR into your daily routine can significantly enhance its effectiveness in managing social anxiety. Here are some tips on when and where to practice:

1. **Morning Routine**: Incorporate PMR into your morning ritual to start your day with a sense of calm. A brief session can set a positive tone and reduce initial stress levels.

2. **Pre-Social Events**: Use PMR before attending social gatherings or events that trigger anxiety. Spending a few minutes practicing relaxation can help alleviate anticipatory stress, making it easier to engage comfortably with others.

3. **Work Breaks**: If your workplace allows, take short breaks to practice PMR during the day. This can help manage work-related stress and maintain overall productivity.

4. **Evening Wind-Down**: Practice PMR before bedtime as part of your nighttime routine. Relaxing your muscles can improve sleep quality by reducing residual tension and promoting a state of tranquility.

5. **Emergency Situations**: In moments of acute anxiety, such as during public speaking or stressful meetings, excuse yourself momentarily, if possible, to perform quick, targeted PMR exercises focusing on areas like your hands or shoulders.

Benefits of PMR

Incorporating Progressive Muscle Relaxation into your anxiety management routine offers numerous physical and psychological benefits:

1. **Reduced Physical Tension**: Regular practice of PMR helps decrease overall muscle tightness. Routinely relaxing muscles prevents the buildup of chronic tension, which can lead to discomfort and fatigue.

2. **Enhanced Sleep Quality**: Practicing PMR, especially in the evening, can improve sleep patterns. Relaxed muscles facilitate falling asleep quicker and enjoying deeper, more restorative sleep.

3. **Lower Anxiety Levels**: Learning to control physical symptoms through PMR often leads to a reduction in general anxiety levels. This creates a positive feedback loop, where reduced tension leads to decreased anxiety, fostering a more relaxed state of being.

4. **Improved Emotional Well-Being**: Successfully using PMR to manage stress can boost self-esteem and reinforce feelings of accomplishment. Building this skill provides a sense of mastery over one's anxiety, contributing to overall emotional resilience.

5. **Physical Health Benefits**: Reducing muscle tension through PMR can also alleviate stress-related physical issues, such as headaches, stomachaches, and muscle pain. Less physical discomfort translates to better overall health and well-being.

Mindful Awareness in Social Settings

Mindful awareness is a practice that invites individuals to be fully present in their experiences, both internally and externally. In the context of social interactions, it involves consciously engaging with others while observing one's thoughts and emotions without judgment. This concept encourages individuals to focus on the current moment, creating space for genuine connection and effective communication.

One practical technique to cultivate mindful awareness in social settings is active listening. This involves truly focusing on what the other person is saying, rather than planning your next response. By maintaining eye contact, nodding, and giving verbal affirmations such as *I understand* or *That makes sense*, you demonstrate your engagement and respect. Active listening enhances your comprehension, fosters empathy, and strengthens relationships.

Grounding techniques can help anchor you in the present moment during social interactions. Simple practices like feeling the sensation of your feet on the ground or noticing the texture of an object in your hand can bring your attention back to the current experience. This helps in reducing the anxiety that often accompanies social situations, providing a stable foundation for mindful engagement.

Self-compassion is another essential element in practicing mindful awareness. Social interactions can trigger self-criticism and fear of judgment. Treating yourself with kindness and understanding can alleviate some of these pressures. Acknowledge your feelings without harsh critique and remind yourself that it's okay to feel anxious. Practicing self-compassion allows you to approach social situations with greater ease and confidence.

Awareness of body language is crucial in non-verbal communication. Your posture, facial expressions, and gestures convey messages just as much as your words do. Being mindful of your body language can help you communicate more effectively and read the cues of others. For instance, maintaining an open posture by uncrossing your arms and making appropriate eye contact can make you appear more approachable and engaged. Conversely, noticing when someone else is exhibiting closed body language can alert you to potential discomfort, prompting you to adjust your approach.

Observing other people's body language is equally important. Non-verbal cues, such as a smile or fidgeting hands, can provide insights into their emotions and thoughts. Recognizing these signals allows you to respond appropriately, fostering better understanding and connection. When you notice signs of discomfort or disengagement, you can address these concerns directly or subtly adjust your behavior to put the other person at ease.

Reflective practices after social interactions are valuable for personal growth and enhancing future engagements. Taking time to reflect on positive experiences can reinforce successful behaviors and boost your confidence. After a social event, consider journaling about the interaction. Reflect on what went well and why, as well as areas where you felt anxious or uncomfortable. This practice helps you identify patterns in your behavior and thought processes, enabling you to make conscious adjustments in future interactions.

Guiding readers to monitor their progress through reflection is also beneficial. Set aside regular periods to assess how your social skills are evolving. Are you becoming more comfortable in conversations? Are you able to remain present and engaged for longer periods? Tracking your evolution highlights your improvements and motivates you to continue practicing mindful awareness.

To integrate these elements, consider a real-life scenario. Imagine attending a networking event where you feel particularly anxious. Begin by grounding yourself—feel the floor beneath your feet and take a few deep breaths. While engaging in conversation, practice active listening by focusing entirely on the speaker, nodding, and offering affirmations. Be mindful of your body language, ensuring it is open and inviting. Observe the other person's non-verbal cues to gauge their comfort level and adjust your approach accordingly. After the event, take time to reflect on your experiences, noting which strategies helped you stay present and identifying areas for improvement.

A concrete example of applying mindful awareness could be during a family gathering. These events can often trigger stress or anxiety due to the complex dynamics involved. Before the gathering, set an intention to remain mindful throughout the event. During conversations, focus intently on each family member's words, showing genuine interest and empathy. Be aware of your body language, aiming to project warmth and openness. Notice the non-verbal cues from your relatives, and if you detect any tension, gently steer the conversation to a more relaxed topic. After the gathering, reflect on the connections you made and the moments where you successfully stayed present despite any internal anxieties.

This chapter examined several mindfulness and relaxation techniques specifically designed to manage anxiety in social situations. Diaphragmatic breathing involves taking deep, calming breaths from the diaphragm, while the 4-7-8 breathing technique offers a structured method to quickly alleviate acute anxiety. We also discussed square breathing, which combines breath control with visualization for rhythmic focus, and mindful breathing, which promotes present-moment awareness without a strict pattern. Each technique provides unique benefits and can be customized to meet individual needs.

We've also delved into guided meditation practices like visualization techniques and loving-kindness meditation, which promote mental clarity and compassion. Progressive Muscle Relaxation (PMR) provides a systematic approach to release physical tension, and mindful awareness encourages active listening and self-compassion during social interactions. Integrating these techniques into daily routines helps individuals cultivate calmness, enhance emotional resilience, and improve their ability to navigate challenging social settings. Consistent practice of these strategies leads to greater confidence and a more positive social experience.

CHAPTER 6
Building Confidence Through Practice

Building confidence through practice is a journey that involves taking consistent, deliberate steps toward self-improvement. This chapter delves into the essential strategies that can help individuals enhance their self-esteem and ease social anxiety by setting achievable goals. Breaking down large ambitions into smaller, manageable tasks and consistently taking action makes the path to improved confidence clearer and more attainable. Understanding this framework will show readers that building self-assurance is not an insurmountable challenge but rather a series of steps leading to a greater sense of personal accomplishment.

The chapter will explore various methods to foster confidence through gradual exposure to social situations, emphasizing the importance of goal-setting. Readers will learn about SMART Goals, which provide structured objectives that are specific, measurable, achievable, relevant, and time-bound. The discussion will also cover how breaking larger goals into smaller steps can mitigate feelings of being overwhelmed and create a steady progression toward success. Flexibility in adapting goals as skills develop, leveraging supportive tools like planners, and celebrating small victories along the way will also be examined. Additionally, the role of peer support and regular evaluation of progress will be highlighted to ensure continuous improvement and sustained motivation.

Setting Achievable Goals

Establishing a framework for setting realistic and attainable goals is essential for building confidence in social situations. This process begins with understanding the importance of SMART Goals, which provide structured objectives that are specific, measurable, achievable, relevant, and time-bound.

SMART Goals are crucial because they help individuals create clear and practical objectives that can be visualized as steps toward success. For example, rather than setting a vague goal like *I want to be more confident*, a SMART Goal would be *I will initiate at least one conversation with a new colleague at work each day for the next two weeks*. This goal is specific (initiating conversations with colleagues), measurable (one conversation per day), achievable (a reasonable expectation), relevant (directly related to building confidence), and time-bound (within two weeks).

Breaking larger goals into smaller, manageable steps minimizes feelings of being overwhelmed and encourages consistent progress. Consider an individual aiming to improve their public speaking skills. Although the large goal might seem daunting, dividing it into smaller steps, such as practicing speeches in front of a mirror, then in front of family, and gradually to a larger audience, makes the entire process more approachable. Achieving each step builds a sense of accomplishment, which fuels further confidence.

Setting timeframes for goals instills a sense of urgency, motivating individuals to take action. Deadlines prevent procrastination and create a structured plan for achieving objectives. For instance, if someone wants to become more confident in networking events, setting a goal of attending one event per week for three months creates a pressing yet manageable challenge. As a result, the individual is likely to push themselves out of their comfort zone, gaining exposure and experience over time.

Adapting goals as skills develop is another key aspect of this framework. Flexibility in goal-setting promotes resilience and prevents discouragement from setbacks. If an individual initially sets a goal to speak up in meetings twice a week but finds this too challenging, they can adapt the goal to start with once a week, gradually increasing frequency as they become more comfortable. This adaptability ensures that goals remain attainable, reducing the risk of feeling like a failure and maintaining motivation.

When working toward these goals, it's helpful to periodically evaluate progress and make necessary adjustments. Regular assessments allow individuals to reflect on what strategies are effective and which ones need modifications. For instance, if the goal is to engage more in social settings but the initial approach isn't yielding desired results, reflecting and pivoting to new strategies, such as joining interest-based groups or practicing active listening, can rejuvenate efforts and keep momentum going.

Additionally, leveraging supportive tools and resources can greatly enhance the journey of goal attainment. Utilizing planners, calendars, and checklists helps in organizing tasks and tracking progress systematically. According to Hernandez, using a planner can significantly aid in laying out daily, weekly, and monthly goals, ensuring that each objective is intertwined with a timeline that keeps individuals accountable (Hernandez, n.d.). This methodical approach organizes the process and visually represents achievements, offering continuous motivation.

Breaking down goals allows for celebrating small victories along the way. Acknowledging these milestones is crucial as it reinforces the belief in personal capability and fosters a positive feedback loop. For example, if someone's ultimate goal is to lead a group discussion, recognizing and celebrating the achievement of contributing ideas in smaller meetings can boost their confidence and prepare them for bigger challenges. Celebrations can be as simple as treating oneself to something enjoyable or sharing the success with friends and family.

Furthermore, incorporating peer support can greatly benefit the goal-setting process. Sharing goals with friends, mentors, or support groups provides external validation and accountability, creating a network that encourages persistence even when challenges arise. Having peers offer constructive feedback and celebrate achievements can enhance motivation and self-belief.

It's important to note that while the primary focus is on building confidence in social situations, the principles discussed apply broadly to various aspects of life. Whether improving professional skills or pursuing personal interests, establishing a robust goal-setting framework can pave the way for significant achievements.

Incremental Success

Building confidence through gradual practice begins with the notion of starting small. Taking on smaller tasks and challenges can be incredibly effective in easing into bigger, more daunting scenarios over time. This approach makes larger challenges appear less intimidating and helps build momentum as each small success lays a foundation for future achievements.

When individuals experience small wins, it boosts their motivation and sets off a chain reaction of positivity. These incremental successes accumulate, creating a sense of progress and making the path to larger goals seem more attainable. Imagine someone who is afraid of public speaking. They might start by practicing brief presentations to a mirror or close friends. Each successful attempt builds their confidence step by step until speaking in front of a larger audience no longer feels overwhelming.

Recognizing and celebrating these milestones is crucial. Acknowledging achievements, no matter how minor they may seem, reinforces the belief in one's abilities. This reinforcement fosters a positive mindset that encourages further efforts and reduces the likelihood of giving up when faced with difficulties. It's important to take note of these moments and remember them during times of self-doubt. For example, keeping a journal where you record each small victory can serve as a powerful reminder of your capabilities and progress.

Embracing the journey rather than focusing solely on the end results is another key component of building self-confidence through practice. When individuals shift their focus from immediate outcomes to the process itself, they are more likely to appreciate their efforts and learn along the way. This perspective encourages continuous improvement and resilience, as setbacks become opportunities for learning rather than failures. Instead of viewing a less-than-perfect social interaction as a failure, see it as a valuable experience that provides insights for future encounters.

Sharing your goals with a friend or mentor can greatly enhance accountability and support. Discussing your ambitions with someone fosters a sense of responsibility and offers a valuable support system during challenging times. Friends and mentors can provide encouragement, offer constructive feedback, and celebrate your milestones. This community support ensures you're not alone on your journey and delivers essential motivation when obstacles arise.

To put this into practice, consider setting small, achievable goals in various aspects of life. These could range from initiating a conversation with a colleague to joining a small group activity. The key is to start with manageable tasks and gradually increase the level of difficulty. This method will help you build confidence incrementally and prepare you for more significant challenges.

For instance, if your goal is to improve your social interactions, begin by making eye contact and smiling at people you meet throughout the day. Once you feel comfortable with this, move on to greeting them verbally. The next step could be engaging in brief conversations, such as commenting on the weather or asking about their day. Each of these actions is a small step toward building your overall confidence in social situations.

As you progress, keep track of your accomplishments and reflect on how far you've come. Writing down your experiences and feelings after each milestone can help solidify your achievements and remind you of your growth. This reflective practice boosts morale and provides valuable insights that can guide future efforts.

Moreover, don't hesitate to seek feedback from those around you. Constructive criticism from trusted friends or mentors can highlight areas for improvement and offer new perspectives. Positive feedback, on the other hand, reinforces your strengths and successes. Both types of feedback contribute to a well-rounded understanding of your progress and help you identify the next steps in your journey.

In addition to individual efforts, group activities can also play a vital role in building confidence. Participating in team sports, joining clubs, or volunteering for group projects allows for shared experiences and collective growth. These settings provide opportunities to practice social skills in a supportive environment while contributing to a common goal. The camaraderie within groups can enhance your sense of belonging and encourage you to step out of your comfort zone.

Furthermore, it's essential to remain patient and kind to yourself throughout this process. Building confidence is not an overnight transformation; it requires time, effort, and persistence. There will be setbacks and challenges along the way, but these should be viewed as integral parts of the journey. Remember that every small step forward is progress, even if it doesn't always feel like it.

Gradual Exposure to Feared Situations

To demystify the process of facing feared social situations in a structured and manageable way, it is crucial to understand and implement several effective strategies. The goal is to make these encounters less intimidating and more approachable by breaking down the steps involved and gradually increasing exposure.

Exposure Hierarchy

One of the fundamental concepts in overcoming social anxiety is using an exposure hierarchy. This method involves ranking social fears from the least to the most distressing and tackling them systematically. For instance, if you fear public speaking, you might start with speaking in front of a mirror, then progress to speaking in front of a friend, and eventually work up to presenting in front of a small group. Beginning with less challenging tasks allows you to build confidence incrementally. Each successful encounter reinforces your ability to handle increasingly difficult situations, reducing overall anxiety over time.

Start by listing your fears and assigning a distress rating to each one on a scale from 1 to 10. Then, structure your practice sessions accordingly. It's important to move at a comfortable pace, ensuring that each step builds on the last without feeling overwhelming. Consistent practice and gradual exposure help desensitize anxiety triggers, making previously daunting situations more manageable.

Visualization Techniques

Another powerful tool in reducing anxiety is visualization. This technique involves mentally rehearsing positive outcomes in social situations before they occur. Visualization helps create a mental blueprint for how you want interactions to unfold, making real-life scenarios feel more familiar and less threatening.

Before attending a social event, spend a few minutes imagining yourself there. Picture engaging confidently in conversations, smiling, and receiving positive responses. Focus on the sensory details: what you'll see, hear, and feel. This mental rehearsal primes your brain for success and diminishes the anticipatory anxiety often associated with such events. Regular practice of visualization can lead to increased self-assurance and decreased fear when facing social interactions.

Reflecting Through Journaling

Keeping a journal is another effective strategy for managing social anxiety. Journaling encourages reflection on your experiences, helping you identify patterns and assess progress. Recording your thoughts, feelings, and reactions to different social situations provides insights into the triggers of your anxiety and the effectiveness of various coping strategies. After each social encounter, take a few moments to jot down your observations. Consider what went well, what triggered your anxiety, and how you responded. Over time, this reflective practice allows you to recognize improvements and pinpoint areas needing further attention. Additionally, journaling serves as a safe outlet for expressing emotions, which can be therapeutic and contribute to emotional regulation.

Peer Support

Engaging in exposure exercises with peers can provide significant benefits. Working alongside others who share similar challenges creates a supportive and relaxed environment conducive to growth. Peer support offers immediate feedback, encouragement, and a sense of camaraderie, reducing feelings of isolation.

Participate in group therapy sessions or join support groups where members practice social interactions together. These settings allow you to receive constructive feedback and observe different approaches to handling anxiety-inducing situations. The collective effort fosters a learning community where everyone supports one another's progress, making it easier to face fears and celebrate achievements.

Seeking Feedback and Improvement

Highlighting the importance of constructive feedback in refining social skills and boosting self-confidence is a critical step toward personal development. Constructive criticism, unlike its negative counterpart, is aimed at providing specific, actionable, and supportive guidance. Understanding this distinction can shift an individual's mindset from one of discouragement to one of growth.

Constructive criticism is more than just pointing out what went wrong; it provides clear steps on how to improve. Imagine you are practicing a speech and a friend suggests that you speak slower in certain parts for better emphasis. This kind of advice is immediate, tangible, and focused on a particular aspect of your performance, making it easier for you to take action and see progress. Recognizing constructive criticism as a tool for improvement rather than a personal attack is key to developing this growth-oriented mindset.

Role-playing is another effective method for refining social skills. It simulates real-life conversations, allowing you to experiment with different approaches in a safe and controlled environment. For example, if small talk makes you anxious, you could role-play various scenarios with a trusted friend or therapist. This helps you practice and receive immediate feedback. Over time, these simulated experiences build your confidence in handling similar situations in the real world.

Engaging in peer review sessions can further enhance your social skills. Much like how writers and students benefit from peer reviews of their work, social skill practitioners can gain valuable insights through community feedback. Joining a peer group focused on improving social skills offers a supportive space where everyone is working toward the same goal. In such settings, individuals share experiences, exchange constructive criticism, and provide mutual encouragement. The communal aspect of peer review fosters a sense of belonging and shared learning, which is particularly beneficial for those struggling with social anxiety.

Self-assessment is another crucial component alongside external feedback. Evaluating your actions and responses to various social situations enhances self-awareness and helps identify specific areas for improvement. Regular reflection on your interactions allows you to become more attuned to your social behavior. Combining self-assessment with external feedback creates a comprehensive framework for targeted skill-building. For instance, self-assessment might reveal a tendency to interrupt others during conversations. External feedback from friends or mentors can then offer strategies to mitigate this habit, such as practicing active listening techniques.

The combination of self-assessment and external feedback is powerful because it encourages continuous learning and adaptation. While external feedback can highlight areas you might overlook, self-assessment ensures that you remain actively engaged in your personal growth journey. Balancing these two forms of feedback helps create a well-rounded perspective on your progress and keeps you motivated to improve.

Moreover, integrating these practices into your daily routine can make a significant difference. Set aside time each week for role-playing exercises, joining peer review sessions, or engaging in self-assessment activities. Consistency is key, as social competence, like any other skill, requires regular practice and dedication. Making these activities a part of your routine gradually builds your confidence and ease in social situations.

It's also essential to approach constructive feedback with an open mind. Sometimes, hearing about our shortcomings can be challenging, especially when we're already feeling vulnerable. However, it's important to remember that the purpose of constructive criticism is to help us grow. Viewing feedback as an opportunity for improvement rather than a judgment of our worth helps maintain a positive attitude toward personal development.

Celebrating Small Victories

Celebrating small victories is essential for building lasting confidence, especially for those dealing with social anxiety. Recognizing and commemorating these modest achievements creates a positive reinforcement loop that motivates further efforts. When you begin to value these small wins, your brain releases dopamine, a neurotransmitter linked to pleasure and reward. This natural high boosts your mood and encourages you to continue taking steps toward your goals.

Developing a routine celebration ritual can significantly reinforce these positive habits. One effective method is journaling. Writing down your daily successes, no matter how minor they seem, creates a tangible record of your progress. For example, jotting down a successful conversation you initiated at a social event helps solidify the memory and reinforces the behavior. Over time, reviewing your journal allows you to see the accumulation of victories, bolstering your confidence.

Another powerful ritual is sharing your achievements with friends or family. This practice validates your experiences and fosters a supportive environment. For instance, texting a friend about completing a challenging task at work or overcoming a social hurdle can provide immediate positive feedback. Sharing accomplishments within trusted circles promotes connection and mutual support, which are crucial for emotional well-being.

Creating vision boards is an additional effective tool for this process. Serving as visual reminders of your progress and aspirations, vision boards keep you focused and inspired. Including images and words that represent your goals and achievements creates a constant source of motivation. Each time you add a new accomplishment to the board, it reinforces the idea that you are moving forward, no matter the pace. This visual affirmation can be particularly uplifting during challenging times, reminding you of past successes and potential future triumphs.

It's important to note that the act of celebrating doesn't need to be grand or elaborate. Simple gestures like treating yourself to a favorite snack, taking a relaxing walk or even giving yourself a mental high-five can be incredibly effective. The key is consistency. Regularly acknowledging your progress, no matter how small, keeps the momentum going. It shifts your focus from what you haven't achieved yet to what you have already accomplished, thereby nurturing a more positive mindset.

Incorporating these practices into daily life requires intention and mindfulness. Setting aside time each day or week for these rituals ensures that they become ingrained habits. For example, you might allocate five minutes each evening to journal about your day's achievements or schedule a weekly coffee catch-up with a friend to discuss mutual progress. These small commitments make the practice sustainable and enjoyable rather than burdensome.

Moreover, engaging in these rituals can have a ripple effect on your broader social interactions. As you become more accustomed to recognizing and celebrating your own achievements, you may find it easier to acknowledge and appreciate the successes of others. This mutual exchange of positivity strengthens relationships and builds a network of support and encouragement. Celebrating together creates a sense of community and shared growth, which can be particularly beneficial for those who struggle with social anxiety.

To illustrate, imagine you've been working on improving your public speaking skills. Initially, the thought of speaking in front of a group, no matter how small, was daunting. However, by consistently practicing and celebrating each step—whether it's speaking up in meetings, participating in discussions, or eventually giving a short presentation—you build confidence incrementally. Sharing your progress with colleagues or friends can garner supportive feedback and encouragement, further boosting your self-esteem.

The cumulative effect of these practices is profound. Each small victory celebrated contributes to a growing bank of positive experiences that reshape your self-perception. You begin to view challenges not as insurmountable obstacles but as opportunities for growth and achievement. This shift in perspective is pivotal for building lasting confidence and reducing social anxiety.

In this chapter, we explored practical methods for building self-confidence through thoughtful and incremental practice. Setting achievable goals allows individuals to approach social situations with greater ease and assurance. The chapter outlines steps such as establishing SMART Goals and breaking down larger objectives into smaller, manageable tasks to create a structured yet adaptable framework for personal growth. These tools are designed to help readers gradually build their confidence, celebrate small victories, and adjust their strategies as they advance. In addition to goal-setting, the chapter highlights the importance of consistent evaluation and support. Regularly reflecting on achievements and seeking constructive feedback enables individuals to refine their approach and stay motivated. Tools like planners, journaling, and peer support networks further support the journey toward enhanced self-esteem and reduced anxiety. Embracing these practices fosters resilience and promotes lasting change in social interactions and beyond.

CHAPTER 7
Improving Communication Skills

Enhancing communication skills can be a transformative experience for those striving to overcome social anxiety. This journey involves learning various techniques that improve conversations and boost confidence and foster more positive social interactions. Whether in personal or professional settings, effective communication is crucial for building meaningful relationships, minimizing misunderstandings, and feeling more comfortable with others.

In this chapter, readers will discover essential strategies for honing their active listening skills, a cornerstone of successful interactions. Techniques such as nodding, summarizing, and asking clarifying questions will be explored to ensure messages are received clearly and accurately. The chapter will also cover verbal communication strategies, emphasizing the importance of clarity and conciseness, the use of open-ended questions, and the practice of tone and pacing. Additionally, readers will learn about non-verbal communication cues, such as maintaining positive body language, making appropriate eye contact, and being aware of personal space. Lastly, the chapter provides practical advice for overcoming the fear of public speaking, including tips on preparation, visualization exercises, and focusing on audience engagement. With these comprehensive insights, individuals will gain the practical tools needed to navigate social situations with greater confidence and ease.

Active Listening Techniques

Active listening plays a vital role in fostering genuine connections and easing anxiety in conversations. Fully concentrating on the speaker and ensuring their message is received clearly and accurately can lead to significant improvements in social interactions.

Active listening requires more than just hearing words; it demands engaging with the speaker through various techniques like nodding, summarizing, and asking clarifying questions. Nodding indicates understanding and encourages the speaker to continue, while summarizing confirms that the listener has correctly interpreted the essence of the conversation. Asking clarifying questions ensures any points of confusion are addressed promptly, demonstrating a sincere effort to comprehend the speaker's message. These actions collectively show the speaker that their words are valued, which can lighten social tension and pave the way for more meaningful dialogue.

Practicing these active listening strategies might initially feel unnatural, but regular practice can make these techniques second nature. Like any other skill, being good at active listening takes time and patience. It is important not to get discouraged if it does not come easily at first. With frequent practice, responsiveness becomes more familiar, creating a more relaxed environment over time. As this familiarity grows, the anxiety associated with social interactions diminishes, making communication more enjoyable and less stressful.

Addressing distractions and personal biases is another vital aspect of active listening. Distractions can range from a noisy environment to intrusive thoughts that divert attention away from the conversation. To counter these, individuals should strive to create a conducive environment for listening, free from potential interruptions. This might involve selecting quieter places for discussions or consciously setting aside worries and mental distractions during interactions.

Personal biases can also impede effective listening by causing premature judgments about the speaker or their message. Being aware of these biases and actively working to set them aside allows for more open and unbiased communication. This heightened self-awareness fosters better understanding and empathy, enhancing the quality of social interactions.

A practical example can be seen in professional settings, where clear and empathetic communication often leads to improved teamwork and outcomes. For instance, healthcare professionals who master active listening can reduce miscommunications and errors, thereby enhancing patient care and team collaboration. In such high-stress environments, the clarity and completeness brought about by active listening are invaluable assets.

Equally important is the role of active listening in personal relationships. Whether it's a conversation with a partner, a family member, or a friend, practicing these skills helps build trust and mutual respect. When individuals feel heard and understood, they are more likely to share openly, strengthening the bond between the speaker and the listener. This can be particularly beneficial in emotionally charged situations where the speaker needs support rather than solutions.

Incorporating curiosity into conversations also aids active listening. When genuinely interested in the subject matter, listeners naturally ask more questions and seek deeper understanding. This curiosity-driven approach makes conversations more engaging and informative, benefiting both parties involved. Finding common interests can further enhance this effect, as shared passions make it easier to stay fully engaged and connected.

Understanding when to respectfully exit a conversation is also a part of active listening. If the other person appears disinterested or uncomfortable, gracefully ending the interaction can prevent feelings of annoyance or being unheard. This mindful approach ensures that conversations remain positive experiences for both parties.

For those struggling with active listening due to social anxiety or attention issues, seeking professional help can be beneficial. Mental health professionals offer various interventions, including social skills training and personalized therapy, to address specific challenges. Engaging in these programs can provide structured support and boost confidence in communication skills.

Moreover, continuous practice of active listening techniques can inspire others to do the same. Demonstrating genuine interest and engagement encourages reciprocation, gradually cultivating a culture of attentive and respectful communication within one's social circle.

Active listening is a skill that is developed through intentional practice and dedication, rather than being an innate talent. Its advantages go beyond the moment, enhancing emotional well-being and strengthening social bonds. Embracing active listening can transform communication habits, helping to reduce social anxiety and cultivate a deeper, more empathetic understanding of others.

Effective Verbal Communication Strategies

Effective verbal communication is essential for minimizing misunderstandings and easing social anxiety. This subpoint provides readers with practical techniques to express themselves more clearly and confidently, promoting a more positive and engaging interaction environment.

Clarity and Conciseness

One pivotal aspect of effective verbal communication is clarity and conciseness. Clear and concise speech fosters confidence because a well-structured message is easier to deliver and understand. When speaking, it's essential to focus on the main points and avoid unnecessary details that can cloud the message or lead to confusion. For example, instead of saying, *I believe that it might be a good idea to consider looking into the possibility of improving our methods*, opt for, *We should improve our methods*. This makes the message clearer and projects confidence, which can alleviate some anxiety about the interaction.

Guideline: Practice simplifying your thoughts before speaking. Take a moment to organize your ideas and eliminate superfluous words. Over time, this will become second nature, making your communication more effective and reducing the stress associated with speaking.

Using Open-Ended Questions

Another powerful technique to enhance communication is asking open-ended questions. Unlike closed questions, which can be answered with a simple "yes" or "no," open-ended questions encourage dialogue, allowing deeper interactions and shifting focus away from self-consciousness. For instance, instead of asking, "Did you have a good weekend?" one might ask, "What did you do over the weekend?" This invites the other person to share more about their experience, thus creating a more engaging conversation.

Guideline: Incorporate open-ended questions in your conversations to promote a two-way dialogue. This approach enriches the interaction and takes the pressure off yourself, as it encourages the other person to share more, facilitating a natural flow of conversation.

Practicing Tone and Pace

The tone and pace of one's speech significantly impact how messages are received and can play a crucial role in managing anxiety. A calm tone combined with a controlled pace allows for better reflection during conversations. Speaking too quickly or too loudly may convey nervousness or aggression, whereas a steady tempo and moderate volume can project calmness and confidence. For example, if discussing a complex topic, pausing briefly between key points helps to ensure the listener comprehends the information fully, reducing the likelihood of misunderstandings.

Guideline: Record yourself speaking and listen to the playback to identify areas where you might need to slow down or modulate your tone. This practice can be incredibly revealing and provides a concrete way to make improvements. Over time, adopting a calm tone and measured pace will become more natural, contributing to your overall confidence in conversations.

Emphasizing Storytelling

Sharing personal anecdotes can transform a routine conversation into an engaging and relatable interaction. Personal stories captivate attention and foster emotional connections, making your communications more memorable. For instance, if you're explaining a business concept, illustrating it with a relevant personal experience can make the information more accessible and interesting to the listener. Stories humanize interactions, bridging gaps and making both parties feel more connected.

Communicating effectively is not just about relaying information but also about making the exchange meaningful and engaging. When you share personal experiences, it allows others to see a glimpse of your world, building rapport and trust. However, balance is key; ensure your anecdotes are relevant to the topic at hand so they enhance rather than detract from your main message.

Non-Verbal Communication Cues

Body language plays a crucial role in communication, often speaking louder than words themselves. Harnessing the power of non-verbal cues can significantly boost one's confidence and ease social anxiety, making interactions smoother and more enjoyable.

To begin with, maintaining positive body language is essential for creating a favorable first impression. People often form judgments about others within seconds of meeting them, largely based on non-verbal signals. A welcoming smile, open stance, and relaxed gestures can make an individual appear more approachable and confident. This instant rapport helps to reduce anxiety for both parties involved in the interaction, making the conversation flow more naturally.

Facial expressions and eye contact are pivotal in promoting connection and attentiveness. When engaging with someone, maintaining appropriate facial expressions demonstrates empathy and understanding. For example, a genuine smile can convey warmth and friendliness, while nodding shows agreement or interest. Eye contact, on the other hand, is a powerful tool in non-verbal communication. It signals attention and respect, reducing self-focus and helping to forge a deeper connection with the other person. Consistent eye contact also reassures the listener that their message is being received and valued. (Segal et al., 2023) suggests that maintaining eye contact is instrumental in effective communication and building strong interpersonal connections.

Good posture and mindful awareness of personal space are other critical aspects of body language that contribute to comfort and safety in interactions. Standing or sitting upright with shoulders back conveys confidence and self-assuredness. Slouching, conversely, can give off an impression of insecurity or disinterest. It's equally important to be aware of personal space. Invading someone's personal space can cause discomfort and increase anxiety levels in both parties. Respecting boundaries will help create a sense of security, making interactions more pleasant and less stressful.

Moreover, mirroring the body language of others can create a sense of familiarity and comfort, reducing tension and fostering empathy. Mirroring involves subtly mimicking the gestures, posture, and movements of the person you are speaking with. This technique can make the other person feel understood and connected on a deeper level. It's an unconscious way of building rapport and demonstrating empathy. However, it's vital to practice this subtly to avoid coming across as mocking or insincere. Studies have shown that when people feel mirrored, they are more likely to trust and engage positively in the conversation.

Grasping and applying the principles of non-verbal communication can bring about significant benefits, especially for those dealing with social anxiety. Adopting positive body language can be transformative, helping individuals shift their focus away from internal anxieties and become more in tune with the dynamics of their interactions. This increased awareness often leads to more meaningful and enjoyable social experiences.

Take John, for example, who struggles with social anxiety and is attending a networking event. By deliberately maintaining an open posture, making eye contact, and subtly mirroring the gestures of those he's speaking with, John can project a sense of confidence and approachability. These non-verbal cues help him feel more at ease and encourage others to engage with him positively. Over time, these constructive interactions can bolster John's self-assurance, gradually reducing his social anxiety.

Additionally, mental health professionals can use these principles to support their clients dealing with social anxiety. Therapists and counselors might incorporate role-playing exercises into their sessions, where clients practice maintaining eye contact, using open body language, and mirroring behaviors. These simulated interactions can serve as safe environments for individuals to experiment with and refine their non-verbal communication skills before applying them in real-world scenarios.

Regularly practicing these techniques can greatly enhance one's ability to navigate social situations with confidence. Positive body language often acts as a self-fulfilling prophecy—by presenting oneself confidently, a person starts to feel more confident internally. This internal shift helps to reduce self-doubt and anxiety, making social interactions more enjoyable and fulfilling.

For those interested in personal development and self-help, mastering non-verbal communication offers a tangible way to enhance social skills and emotional well-being. Books, seminars, and workshops focused on communication skills often highlight the importance of body language.

Engaging with such resources can provide valuable insights and practical strategies to improve non-verbal communication.

Overcoming Fear of Public Speaking

Public speaking is a major trigger for social anxiety, but by understanding and addressing common fears, this daunting task can become more manageable. Recognizing that many people experience anxiety when speaking in public helps normalize these feelings. Common fears include making mistakes, being judged by the audience, forgetting parts of the speech, or displaying visible signs of nervousness like trembling hands or a shaky voice. Acknowledging these shared concerns can help individuals feel less isolated and more accepted, which can greatly reduce performance anxiety.

Thorough preparation and practice are essential strategies for combating the fear of public speaking. When speakers know their material well, it reduces the likelihood of errors and enhances their ability to recover quickly if they do occur. This expertise on the topic boosts confidence and diminishes uncertainty. Preparation should involve organizing the content meticulously, including the use of visual aids or notes to stay on track during the presentation. Additionally, rehearsing the speech multiple times, particularly in front of others, allows speakers to refine their delivery and receive constructive feedback. Practicing in different environments can also help acclimate the speaker to various settings, further reducing anxiety. These steps imbue the speaker with a sense of control and mastery over their presentation (Sawchuk, 2017).

Visualization exercises offer another powerful tool for alleviating public speaking anxiety. These exercises involve mentally rehearsing the presentation in a positive light. For instance, speakers can visualize themselves delivering their speech confidently, receiving applause, and connecting effectively with the audience. This mental preparation trains the brain to anticipate success rather than failure, shifting the focus from fear to a positive outcome. Visualization can be particularly effective when combined with other relaxation techniques such as deep breathing, which calms the mind and body. By repeatedly visualizing successful outcomes, speakers can build self-assurance and decrease negative thoughts associated with their social performance (Cuncic, 2019).

Focusing on the audience rather than concentrating on personal insecurities can significantly improve the public speaking experience. When speakers shift their attention outward, they become more attuned to the needs and reactions of their listeners. Engaging with the audience through eye contact, gestures, and interactive questions fosters a connection that makes the experience more collaborative and less intimidating. Understanding that the audience is there to listen and learn, rather than criticize, can alleviate self-doubt. Moreover, audience members often empathize with speakers and root for their success, especially if they notice signs of nervousness. By concentrating on delivering value to the audience, speakers can divert their attention from internal fears and enhance their overall presence and effectiveness.

In this chapter, we delved into powerful techniques designed to elevate communication skills, with a spotlight on the transformative impact of active listening. Engaging mindfully with speakers, nodding in understanding, and asking clarifying questions can revolutionize interactions and ease social anxiety. Overcoming common barriers like distractions and biases becomes a gateway to more open and empathetic conversations. As these techniques are practiced regularly, they naturally become ingrained, leading to more confident and fulfilling social exchanges.

We also uncovered dynamic verbal communication strategies that bring clarity and conciseness to conversations. Open-ended questions spark deeper discussions, while the right tone and pacing can make every interaction more engaging. Personal anecdotes, combined with well-managed non-verbal cues like body language and eye contact, help to break down social anxiety and build meaningful connections. For those facing the challenge of public speaking, preparation, and visualization exercises unlock a path to confidence. These practical tools are the key to transforming communication patterns, reducing social anxiety, and enriching social experiences.

CHAPTER 8
Support Systems and Professional Help

Support systems and professional assistance are crucial in managing social anxiety. Although navigating social anxiety can be overwhelming, a dependable network of supportive individuals can make a significant impact. This chapter examines how friends and family offer essential emotional support and practical help, creating a safe environment that encourages understanding and empathy. Building a strong support network involves identifying those who positively contribute to one's well-being and recognizing individuals who might unintentionally increase anxiety.

The chapter also explores the value of participating in community activities and how they can enhance one's support system. Establishing clear boundaries to protect emotional health and seeking professional help from therapists and counselors are discussed as effective strategies. Integrating personal relationships with structured professional guidance provides a comprehensive approach to managing social anxiety. This chapter presents a balanced perspective on utilizing both personal and professional support systems to enhance overall quality of life.

Building a Supportive Network

A strong support network is vital in managing social anxiety, providing both emotional encouragement and practical assistance. Friends and family play a crucial role in this process, offering understanding, empathy, and validation to those experiencing social anxiety. Their support can make an individual feel less isolated and more secure in facing their fears.

Assessing who is supportive versus who may trigger anxiety is essential for organizing interactions that are beneficial rather than detrimental. Identifying trustworthy individuals who genuinely understand and provide comfort helps create a safe space for expressing emotions without judgment. Those who consistently offer negative feedback or dismissive attitudes should be noted as potential sources of increased anxiety. Having open dialogues with supportive individuals about one's experiences and triggers can foster deeper connections and trust. This honest communication ensures that friends and family know how best to provide assistance during anxious moments.

Engaging in activities that foster socialization, such as hobbies or volunteering, is another effective way to build relationships and manage social anxiety. Participating in group activities allows individuals to practice social skills and gradually become more comfortable in social settings. These activities also provide opportunities to connect with like-minded people, forming new friendships that can further expand one's support network. For instance, joining a book club or taking a cooking class enhances personal interests and encourages interaction in a low-pressure environment.

Establishing boundaries is crucial for safeguarding emotional well-being during challenging times. Clear boundaries help individuals manage their energy levels and reduce the risk of becoming overwhelmed by social obligations. It's important to communicate these boundaries to friends and family, ensuring they understand and respect the need for personal space when required.

In addition to fostering close relationships, having a broad support system within the community can be beneficial. Community groups, local clubs, and support organizations offer additional layers of support, allowing individuals to interact with others who share similar experiences and challenges. Engaging in community activities provides a sense of belonging and enhances self-esteem, knowing there are others who truly understand the struggles of social anxiety.

Furthermore, professional support, including therapists and counselors, can complement personal support networks. Professionals provide structured guidance, teach coping strategies, and offer tools tailored to individual needs. Regular sessions with a mental health professional ensure that progress is monitored and adjustments are made as needed. This specialized support can significantly alleviate the symptoms of social anxiety and improve overall quality of life.

Creating a balance between relying on friends and family and seeking professional help is essential. While personal relationships offer emotional warmth and immediate comfort, professionals bring expertise and objectivity to address deeper issues. Combining both sources of support forms a comprehensive approach to managing social anxiety effectively.

Role of Therapy and Counseling

Therapy and counseling are crucial components in managing social anxiety. They provide a structured environment where individuals can explore their thoughts, behaviors, and emotions under the guidance of trained professionals. Various therapeutic modalities offer distinct methods to address anxiety issues from different angles, making therapy a versatile tool in combating social anxiety.

One of the most widely recognized therapies for social anxiety is Cognitive-behavioral therapy (CBT). Originating from the works of psychologists such as Albert Ellis and Aaron T. Beck, CBT focuses on changing maladaptive thought patterns that contribute to anxiety. It employs cognitive restructuring to help individuals identify and challenge negative thoughts, replacing them with more realistic and constructive ones. The effectiveness of CBT in treating various anxiety disorders, including social anxiety, has been well-documented. CBT is often seen as a short-term, skills-focused treatment aimed at providing immediate relief and long-term coping strategies (Kaczkurkin & Foa, 2018).

Exposure therapy, a key component of CBT, involves gradually confronting anxiety-provoking situations in a controlled setting. This approach helps individuals increase their tolerance to feared scenarios by facing them rather than avoiding them. Based on the emotional processing theory, exposure therapy suggests that repeated exposure to fear-inducing stimuli can lessen the intensity of the fear response over time. Engaging in exposure exercises during therapy sessions and as part of homework assignments can significantly alleviate social anxiety symptoms by desensitizing individuals to their fears (Cohen, 2016).

Behavioral experiments are also integral to CBT for social anxiety. These experiments allow individuals to test their "hot thoughts" or anxiety-inducing beliefs against real-life evidence. Engaging in behavioral experiments can help clients see that their fears are often exaggerated and not grounded in reality. For instance, someone who fears public speaking might practice giving a short speech in a therapy session or in front of a small group to gather evidence that contradicts their fear of being ridiculed. Such experiments foster self-confidence and provide concrete experiences that counteract irrational fears (Cohen, 2016).

Searching for a therapist with a specialization in anxiety disorders can significantly enhance the healing process. A specialized therapist will have in-depth knowledge and experience in handling social anxiety, making them better equipped to tailor treatments to the individual's specific needs. Professional associations like the Anxiety and Depression Association of America (ADAA) often provide directories of therapists who specialize in anxiety disorders, making it easier for individuals to find qualified professionals.

Therapy equips individuals with a variety of tools and coping strategies tailored to address specific anxieties and triggers. These strategies encompass relaxation techniques, mindfulness practices, assertiveness training, and problem-solving skills. For example, mindfulness encourages focusing on the present moment and distancing oneself from anxious thoughts, which helps reduce their influence. Assertiveness training enables those with social anxiety to communicate their needs and opinions confidently, free from fear of judgment. With these tools, therapy fosters proactive management of anxiety, leading to improved social interactions and a higher overall quality of life.

Regular sessions with a therapist can help maintain progress and accountability. Consistent therapy sessions create a sense of routine and commitment, encouraging individuals to stay focused on their therapeutic goals. Regular check-ins with a therapist provide opportunities to discuss challenges, celebrate successes, and adjust treatment plans as needed. This ongoing support fosters a sustained effort toward overcoming social anxiety and prevents relapse. Accountability also plays a significant role in reinforcing healthy habits and ensuring that individuals continue to apply the coping strategies learned in therapy.

Group therapy offers an additional layer of support for individuals dealing with social anxiety. In a group setting, participants realize they are not alone in their struggles and can share their experiences in a safe and supportive environment. Group therapy provides a unique opportunity to practice social interactions in a controlled setting, reducing the fear of judgment. The camaraderie among group members enhances motivation and encourages consistent attendance, contributing to long-term success in managing social anxiety.

Group Therapy Benefits

Group therapy can be a powerful tool in enhancing feelings of understanding and camaraderie among individuals with social anxiety. One of the most profound benefits of group settings is the realization that participants are not alone in their struggles. Social anxiety often creates an isolating experience, where individuals feel like their challenges are unique or misunderstood by others. In a group therapy session, members hear stories that mirror their own experiences. This mutual understanding fosters a sense of belonging and helps alleviate feelings of isolation. Knowing that others face similar issues can be incredibly validating and reassuring, providing emotional relief and encouragement.

The controlled environment of group therapy offers a unique setting to practice social interactions without fear of judgment. This is especially crucial for those who find social situations daunting and fraught with anxiety. In these sessions, participants engage in conversations, role-playing, and other activities designed to enhance their social skills. The supportive atmosphere allows them to experiment with new behaviors, make mistakes, and learn from them without the fear of harsh criticism or rejection. Practicing in this safe space helps individuals build confidence in their social abilities, which they can then transfer to real-world situations.

Moreover, being part of a group provides accountability and encourages consistent attendance. When individuals know they have a regular meeting with others who share their experiences, they are more likely to stay committed to attending sessions and working toward their personal goals. This sense of community promotes a sustained effort toward self-improvement. Peer support within the group can be a motivating factor, as members encourage each other to set and achieve targets, share techniques that have worked for them, and celebrate successes, no matter how small.

Trained facilitators play a key role in guiding group discussions. These professionals bring valuable insights and techniques to manage anxiety collectively. They create a structured framework for the sessions, ensuring that discussions remain focused and productive. Facilitators are skilled at fostering an inclusive environment where everyone feels comfortable sharing their thoughts and experiences. They also introduce evidence-based strategies and therapeutic exercises tailored to the needs of the group. For instance, cognitive-behavioral techniques might be employed to help participants reframe negative thought patterns, while relaxation exercises can be used to reduce physical symptoms of anxiety.

The collective exploration of emotions and thoughts in a group setting allows participants to offer each other empathy, understanding, and validation. This dynamic can be particularly beneficial, as it creates a network of mutual support. Group members often find comfort in knowing that their vulnerabilities are shared by others. This mutual support system helps to normalize their experiences and diminishes the stigma associated with social anxiety. When individuals see others facing similar challenges and making progress, it can inspire hope and motivate them to persevere in their own journey.

Group therapy also brings together diverse perspectives and insights. Participants come from various backgrounds, ages, and life experiences, enriching the therapeutic process. Hearing different viewpoints on coping mechanisms and problem-solving can provide new strategies and inspiration. For example, someone might share how mindfulness meditation has helped them manage anxiety, prompting others to try the technique. This exchange of ideas broadens the range of tools available to each member, enhancing their ability to manage social anxiety effectively.

Additionally, group therapy sessions serve as a microcosm of real-life social interactions. The group setting mimics various social scenarios, allowing participants to practice essential social skills such as active listening, assertiveness, and conflict resolution. These interactions provide immediate feedback and reinforcement, helping individuals refine their skills in a practical context. Over time, repeated practice in a supportive environment leads to greater confidence and competence in handling social situations outside the therapy room.

Peer support extends beyond the therapy sessions, creating a lasting network of connections. Many groups encourage members to stay in touch between sessions, offering additional opportunities for support and accountability. This ongoing contact can be especially valuable during challenging times, providing a safety net of understanding friends who can offer advice, encouragement, or simply a listening ear. The friendships formed in group therapy can become a crucial part of an individual's long-term support system.

Utilizing Online Resources and Support Groups

Online platforms have become incredibly valuable in managing social anxiety, particularly for those who may find face-to-face interactions overwhelming. The digital age has facilitated numerous avenues where individuals can seek help and support anonymously, comfortably, and from the safety of their homes.

Virtual support groups are a pivotal component in the arsenal against social anxiety. These online communities provide a sense of belonging without the pressure of in-person meetings. For many, participating in a virtual support group can be easier as it removes the stress of physical presence. Engaging with others through video calls or chat rooms allows participants to share their experiences, ask questions, and offer encouragement in a controlled environment tailored to their comfort levels. These groups often include people who have similar struggles, which fosters a sense of camaraderie and mutual understanding that is crucial for emotional support.

Furthermore, various websites and apps are dedicated to offering resources specifically designed for those dealing with social anxiety. These platforms host a plethora of articles, videos, and mindfulness exercises aimed at providing education, coping strategies, and self-help tools. The availability of such content ensures that users can access information when they need it, empowering them to take proactive steps in managing their anxiety. Resources such as guided meditation videos, breathing exercises, and educational articles about social anxiety can be lifesavers for individuals looking to better understand and cope with their condition.

Teletherapy has also seen a significant rise in popularity, making mental health services more accessible than ever before. This form of therapy allows individuals to engage with licensed professionals remotely through video calls or voice chats, eliminating the need for physical travel and reducing the anxiety associated with visiting a therapist's office. Teletherapy sessions can be arranged at times that are convenient for the client, creating a flexible and adaptable solution for those with busy schedules or mobility issues. Furthermore, for some individuals, the ability to speak with a therapist from the comfort of their own home can foster a sense of security and openness that might be harder to achieve in an unfamiliar setting.

Structured online programs add an extra layer of support with organized courses that systematically teach coping techniques. These programs typically feature interactive modules, webinars, and assignments that guide participants through practical strategies for managing social anxiety. A structured approach helps individuals address different facets of their anxiety and track their progress over time. Community forums and group discussions included in these programs offer opportunities for participants to connect with peers on similar journeys, providing validation and motivation through shared experiences.

Managing social anxiety relies heavily on building a supportive network and seeking professional help. Emotional encouragement and practical assistance from family, friends, and trusted individuals create safe spaces for open discussions about experiences and triggers. Expanding this support system through community groups or local clubs offers additional opportunities to connect with others facing similar challenges.

Incorporating professional support, such as therapists or counselors, brings expertise and structured guidance to develop tailored coping strategies. Combining personal and professional support creates a comprehensive approach to managing social anxiety. Personal relationships provide immediate comfort and understanding, while professionals offer objective insights and specialized tools. Regular therapy sessions ensure consistent progress and adjustments, contributing to an improved overall quality of life. Together, these support systems form a balanced framework that enables individuals to navigate social interactions with increased confidence and resilience.

CHAPTER 9
Real-Life Success Stories

Real-life success stories provide invaluable insights into overcoming social anxiety, showcasing the resilience of the human spirit. This chapter presents a collection of remarkable journeys, highlighting the diverse paths individuals have taken to conquer their anxiety. Sharing personal experiences offers readers relatable narratives that deliver both hope and practical guidance for their own challenges. Each story emphasizes the potential for significant personal growth and transformation, even when facing seemingly insurmountable obstacles.

The chapter explores specific experiences with social anxiety, detailing effective strategies and coping mechanisms. Accounts of individuals who have used cognitive-behavioral therapy, assertiveness training, and mindfulness practices illustrate how these methods can help reclaim their lives from anxiety. The stories underscore the importance of professional help and the crucial role of supportive friends and family in the recovery process. Through these real-life examples, readers are inspired and equipped with actionable insights to enhance their social interactions and overall quality of life.

Case Study: Sarah's Journey

Sarah always felt a knot in her stomach when she thought about interacting with others. Her initial challenges with social interactions began in high school, where even mundane tasks like asking for notes from a classmate or answering questions in front of the class became monumental hurdles. Sarah's anxiety grew over time, leading her to avoid social settings altogether. This avoidance had wide-ranging effects on her life. She missed out on numerous opportunities to make friends, join clubs, and participate in activities that could have enriched her young adulthood.

Sarah's social anxiety was most pronounced in situations that involved public speaking and group settings. Attending parties, participating in family gatherings, or even engaging in small talk at work were all exceptionally daunting for her. The emotional and psychological impacts were significant. She constantly feared being judged or rejected, a worry that manifested as sweaty palms, racing thoughts, and an overwhelming urge to flee. As a result, Sarah often found herself isolated, feeling lonely and misunderstood.

The turning point came during a holiday family gathering that Sarah couldn't bring herself to attend. Her absence led to a heartfelt conversation with her mother, who expressed concern for her well-being. This moment of vulnerability prompted Sarah to realize how deeply her anxiety was affecting her life and those around her. Motivated by this wake-up call, she decided it was time to seek help. Supportive friends and family played a crucial role in her journey, encouraging her to consult a mental health professional and explore self-help resources.

Sarah's path to managing her social anxiety involved adopting various strategies and coping mechanisms. One of the first steps she took was to educate herself about social anxiety disorder through books and articles. Reading works like *How to Be Yourself: Quiet Your Inner Critic and Rise Above Social Anxiety* by Ellen Hendriksen provided her with valuable insights into why social anxiety persists and introduced practical methods to alleviate it (Ph.D, 2023).

One of the most impactful techniques Sarah embraced was cognitive-behavioral therapy (CBT). Under the guidance of her therapist, she learned to challenge her negative thought patterns and gradually expose herself to feared situations. For instance, Sarah started small by making eye contact with strangers, then progressed to initiating short conversations. Each success, no matter how minor, built her confidence and reduced her anxiety.

Assertiveness training also proved beneficial. Sarah practiced communicating her needs calmly and respectfully, using "I" statements to express herself without feeling overwhelmed. For example, she would say, "I feel anxious when I'm put on the spot at meetings," which helped her colleagues understand her struggles and offer support. Learning to say "no" when necessary empowered Sarah to set boundaries, reducing stress and enhancing her sense of control (Cuncic, 2020).

Enhancing nonverbal communication skills was a critical step for Sarah. She recognized that her closed-off body language, including crossed arms and averted eye contact, frequently conveyed the wrong impression. Adopting a more open stance—standing tall, making gentle eye contact, and smiling more often—made her appear more approachable. This subtle change in her demeanor significantly improved her interactions, increasing her comfort and confidence in social settings.

To further bolster her verbal communication skills, Sarah focused on becoming a better listener. She practiced asking open-ended questions and sharing personal anecdotes, which helped sustain conversations and foster deeper connections. One useful tip she employed was joining a group discussion by first listening and then contributing relevant comments, such as, "I've also noticed that..." This approach made it easier for her to integrate into conversations without feeling intrusive or anxious.

Deep breathing exercises became a crucial component of Sarah's strategy for managing anxiety. Practicing mindful breathing techniques daily enabled her to keep her body calm even during stressful moments.

Taking deep diaphragmatic breaths—inhale for four seconds and exhale for six—helped lower her heart rate and clear her mind. These exercises proved particularly effective before social events, allowing her to approach them with a more relaxed state of mind (Cuncic, 2020).

Reducing negative thoughts was a key element of Sarah's progress. She realized that much of her anxiety arose from mindreading and personalizing others' behaviors. For instance, she often assumed that people were judging her harshly or finding her presence dull. By challenging and reframing these automatic thoughts, she learned to view social interactions more realistically. Instead of thinking, *Everyone thinks I'm awkward*, she reminded herself, *It's okay to be quiet sometimes; it doesn't mean they dislike me.*

Dealing with setbacks was an inevitable part of Sarah's journey. There were times when her anxiety spiked, and she felt like she was back at square one. However, she learned to view these moments not as failures but as opportunities for growth. By reflecting on what triggered her anxiety and seeking constructive feedback from her therapist, she continually refined her strategies and resilience.

An essential component of Sarah's overall improvement was maintaining a support network. Regularly talking about her feelings with trusted friends and family members offered emotional relief and practical advice. Their encouragement reinforced her belief that she was not alone in this struggle, providing the motivation needed to keep pushing forward.

Sarah's story illustrates that overcoming social anxiety is not a linear process but a series of small, consistent steps. Each strategy she employed—whether cognitive-behavioral techniques, assertiveness training, or deep breathing exercises—contributed to a gradual but meaningful transformation in her life. Her journey underscores the importance of seeking help, embracing vulnerability, and persistently applying practical solutions to manage social anxiety.

Interview With a Therapist

The goal of this section is to offer insights from a professional perspective on the treatment and management of social anxiety. Providing valuable information for those seeking practical solutions, we delve into various therapeutic approaches and techniques that professionals use to guide clients toward recovery.

Therapist's Approach

Introducing the therapist and their method is crucial in understanding how social anxiety is addressed. Therapists often begin by building a strong therapeutic relationship with their clients, creating a safe and non-judgmental environment for them to open up. This rapport is essential for effective therapy as it fosters trust and encourages honest communication.

Therapists use a range of methods tailored to each client's needs. Cognitive-behavioral therapy (CBT) is one such evidence-based approach frequently employed. CBT focuses on identifying and modifying negative thought patterns and behaviors that contribute to social anxiety. Helping clients recognize these thoughts allows therapists to guide them in challenging and replacing irrational beliefs with more balanced and realistic ones.

Common Patterns

Therapists observe certain common patterns among clients with social anxiety. One prevalent pattern is the fear of negative evaluation, where individuals are excessively concerned about being judged or criticized by others. This fear often leads to avoidance behaviors, such as steering clear of social situations or remaining silent in group settings.

Cognitive distortions, another common pattern, involve skewed ways of thinking that fuel anxiety. Examples include catastrophizing (expecting the worst possible outcome), mind-reading (assuming others have negative thoughts about oneself), and all-or-nothing thinking (viewing situations in black-and-white terms). Identifying these distortions is a key step in the therapeutic process, as it allows clients to challenge and reframe their thoughts.

Successful Techniques

Several successful techniques are used in treating social anxiety, with CBT being one of the most effective. Within CBT, therapists utilize cognitive restructuring to address distorted thinking patterns. This involves examining and questioning negative beliefs, gathering evidence for and against them, and developing more balanced perspectives.

Exposure therapy is another vital technique. It involves gradually and systematically exposing clients to feared social situations in a controlled manner. This helps clients build tolerance to anxiety over time and reduces the intensity of their fear responses. Contrary to systematic desensitization, which aims to reduce physical symptoms, exposure therapy emphasizes learning to tolerate and accept anxiety as a normal part of social interactions (Cognitive Behavioral Therapy Los Angeles, 2020).

Mindfulness is a powerful tool in managing social anxiety. Practicing mindfulness allows individuals to become more attuned to their thoughts, emotions, and bodily sensations without judgment. Techniques such as deep breathing and meditation help anchor clients in the present moment, reducing the focus on past mistakes or future worries. Over time, mindfulness fosters a balanced perspective on social situations and enhances emotional regulation.

Behavioral experiments are also beneficial. These involve actively testing the beliefs underlying social anxiety by engaging in real-life situations. For example, attending a social event to gather evidence against the belief that one will be universally disliked. Such experiments help clients develop a more realistic appraisal of social interactions and diminish anxiety-inducing thoughts.

Social skills training is an essential component of therapy for social anxiety. It equips clients with effective communication and interpersonal skills, boosting their confidence in social settings. Practicing scenarios in a supportive environment allows clients to learn how to navigate conversations, maintain eye contact, and express themselves assertively.

Advice for Overcoming Anxiety

Key recommendations for overcoming social anxiety emphasize the importance of professional support, consistent practice, and patience throughout the journey of recovery. Seeking help from a qualified therapist experienced in treating social anxiety can make a significant difference. Professional guidance ensures that interventions are tailored to individual needs and progress is monitored effectively.

Building tolerance to anxiety is a critical aspect of recovery. Accepting anxiety as a natural part of social interactions rather than something to be eradicated can paradoxically reduce its intensity. This involves facing fears gradually through exposure and allowing oneself to experience discomfort without avoiding it. Over time, repeated exposure diminishes anxiety responses and fosters resilience.

Practicing mindfulness regularly can enhance self-awareness and emotional regulation. Simple exercises like mindful breathing, body scans, and meditation can be incorporated into daily routines. These practices help ground individuals in the present moment, reducing rumination on past events or anticipation of future anxieties.

Therapists often recommend challenging and reframing negative thoughts. When clients encounter social anxiety triggers, they are encouraged to identify and question their automatic thoughts. Evaluating whether there is evidence supporting these thoughts and considering alternative interpretations can help reduce the impact of anxiety-inducing beliefs (Raypole, 2021).

Engaging in behavioral experiments empowers clients to test and disprove their fears. For instance, if someone believes they will embarrass themselves at a party, attending the event and observing the actual outcomes can provide valuable corrective experiences. While some interactions may feel awkward, positive encounters often occur, challenging the initial fears and promoting growth.

Developing social skills through deliberate practice can significantly boost confidence. Starting with less intimidating interactions, such as conversing with acquaintances, and gradually progressing to more complex social situations helps individuals build competence and assurance.

Above all, it's important to recognize that overcoming social anxiety is a gradual process. Progress may be slow, and setbacks are a natural part of the journey. Patience, persistence, and self-compassion are essential. Celebrating small victories along the way and acknowledging the effort invested in facing fears can motivate continued growth.

Success Story Compilation

One of the most powerful ways to combat social anxiety is by learning from those who have successfully navigated their own journeys toward overcoming it. Collecting a range of success stories helps foster hope and demonstrates the diverse paths to recovery.

To begin, consider the diverse experiences of individuals from different demographics and backgrounds. Each story is different, offering its own array of challenges and victories. For instance, Stephen Hartzell's journey illustrates how panic disorder and anxiety can spiral out of control under immense stress. His struggle with maintaining a strict calendar, feeling overwhelmed by self-imposed tasks, and experiencing physical symptoms of anxiety highlights a common narrative of overcommitment leading to significant mental health challenges (Hartzell, 2021).

Joseph Ettinger's experience sheds light on the importance of community support. Joining a forum of like-minded individuals provided him with a safe space to share his struggles and find solace in the stories of others. This sense of belonging was crucial in helping him manage his anxiety and find motivation to continue his journey of self-improvement (Browse Personal Stories, n.d.).

From a cultural perspective, Gina Brown's story provides insight into the intersectionality of mental health issues. As a Black or biracial woman, her experiences of depression, bipolar disorder, and anxiety were compounded by societal pressures and racial stereotypes. Despite these additional layers of complexity, her resilience and the supportive role of mental health professionals enabled her to navigate through these challenges.

An illustrative example is Hussain, who found that his OCD and religious obsessions led to isolation during his youth. Channeling his suffering into a passion for helping others, he discovered a sense of purpose and community that was crucial to his recovery. His story highlights the significant impact of aligning personal struggles with broader advocacy efforts to promote connection and healing.

Turning points play a significant role in each individual's journey. For example, Ed Barton's realization that authentic friendships, combined with therapy and medication, were key to his OCD recovery underscores the importance of multifaceted approaches. Similarly, Claire Helmers' breakthrough came when she switched therapists, finding one whose approach resonated deeply with her needs as a competitive runner dealing with anxiety and depression. These key milestones mark critical moments of courage and determination, illustrating the incremental nature of recovery.

Furthermore, the continued growth of these individuals demonstrates how sustaining confidence and practicing ongoing self-care are essential long-term strategies. Natalia Aíza's ability to ignore intrusive thoughts related to her anxiety shows the progress made possible through consistent therapeutic interventions and self-compassion. Julie Streifel's reflections on the valuable lessons learned over two decades of battling social anxiety emphasize the importance of acknowledging and celebrating small victories along the way.

An important aspect of these narratives is the call to action they inspire. By visualizing their own success stories, readers can find hope and encouragement regardless of their starting point. Sarah may find solace in knowing that others who faced similar struggles have managed to rebuild their lives and achieve a sense of normalcy. Mental health professionals can also utilize these stories to better understand the spectrum of experiences and tailor their support accordingly.

For individuals looking for practical solutions to improve their social interactions and quality of life, these stories offer concrete examples of effective strategies. Gradual exposure and facing fears incrementally are common themes across many success stories. For instance, Luciana Valbuena's initial fear and unknown feelings following the birth of her child were gradually overcome by embracing small steps toward connecting with her emotions and seeking appropriate help.

The process of measuring progress and dealing with setbacks is also highlighted in various accounts. Stephen Hartzell's methodical approach to overcoming agoraphobia by challenging himself with specific tasks, such as hiking in Sandia Mountain, showcases the importance of setting achievable goals and recognizing progress incrementally (Hartzell, 2021). Meanwhile, the stories shared within the Anxiety and Depression Association of America community serve as a testament to the effectiveness of peer support and resource sharing

Lessons Learned From Others' Experiences

Common Themes: Identifying trends across different stories, including the universal nature of social anxiety and the importance of self-acceptance

In examining various success stories of individuals who have triumphed over social anxiety, certain common themes emerge. One predominant trend is the universal nature of social anxiety, affecting people regardless of their background or life circumstances. This suggests that social anxiety is a shared human experience, making it easier for readers to relate to these narratives. Another common theme is the importance of self-acceptance. Many individuals in these stories have highlighted how critical it was to accept themselves as they are, flaws and all, before they could begin their journey toward recovery. This acceptance often served as a foundation upon which other strategies could be built.

Practical Techniques: Sharing actionable lessons learned, such as simple exercises and gradual exposure

One of the most valuable insights from these success stories is the practical techniques used by individuals to manage and eventually overcome their social anxiety. Cognitive-behavioral therapy (CBT) is frequently mentioned as a highly effective treatment. CBT helps individuals change their thought patterns and behaviors concerning social interactions. According to clinical psychologist Ramani Durvasula, "If you can help a person change how they think or perceive about a situation, you'll likely change the reactions and the behaviors" (CNN, n.d.).

Another practical technique is gradual exposure. Many individuals found success by slowly exposing themselves to anxiety-provoking situations. For instance, someone who is afraid of public speaking might start by speaking in front of a mirror, then progress to speaking in front of a small group of friends, and finally move on to larger audiences. This step-by-step approach helps desensitize the individual to the fear, making it more manageable over time.

Resilience and Mindset: The mindset shifts that contributed to success, recognizing setbacks as part of the growth process

Mindset plays a crucial role in overcoming social anxiety, and many success stories emphasize the importance of resilience. A significant mindset shift that many individuals experienced was learning to view setbacks not as failures, but as opportunities for growth. This perspective is vital because the journey to overcoming social anxiety is rarely linear. Recognizing that setbacks are part of the process allows individuals to stay committed to their goals even when challenges arise.

Another critical mindset shift is focusing on the present moment rather than worrying about hypothetical future scenarios. This practice, often incorporated into mindfulness techniques, helps individuals become more engaged and less anxious during social interactions. Focusing on the present moment, rather than worrying about potential future events, can help reduce the intensity of anxiety.

Encouragement for the Reader: Reassuring readers that change is possible through time and effort, prompting them to identify their own potential narratives of success

Real-life success stories provide powerful encouragement for readers struggling with social anxiety. These narratives show that change is achievable, but it requires time and consistent effort. Understanding that others have walked this path and emerged stronger can instill hope and motivation in readers.

It's also beneficial for readers to identify their own potential narratives of success. Reflecting on personal goals and envisioning a future where social anxiety is no longer a limiting factor can serve as a powerful motivator. As one story suggested, knowing your talents, capabilities, and worth can significantly boost confidence and self-esteem (Overcoming Low Self-Esteem, 2020). Readers are encouraged to recognize their strengths and work toward incremental progress rather than immediate perfection.

This chapter has highlighted the inspiring journeys of individuals who have effectively managed social anxiety, showcasing various strategies and techniques that aided their recovery. Sarah's story exemplifies the benefits of seeking help and employing cognitive-behavioral therapy, gradual exposure, assertiveness training, and mindfulness practices. Through consistent, small steps, she overcame her fears, developed strong communication skills, and established a supportive network crucial to her progress. The experiences shared in this chapter illustrate that overcoming social anxiety involves both professional guidance and personal determination.

These narratives offer valuable insights for those dealing with social anxiety or supporting someone who does. They emphasize that while the path to recovery can be challenging, it is attainable with patience, persistence, and self-compassion. Techniques such as cognitive restructuring, behavioral experiments, and mindfulness exercises provide actionable strategies for managing and reducing social anxiety. Learning from others' experiences encourages readers to envision their own success stories and take practical steps to enhance their social interactions and overall quality of life.

CHAPTER 10
Maintaining Progress and Looking Forward

Maintaining progress is an ongoing journey that requires dedication and strategic planning. The key to continuous growth, especially beyond overcoming social anxiety, lies in implementing effective strategies that sustain and enhance your development. Understanding the significance of each step you take toward improvement can profoundly impact your trajectory, ensuring that every effort contributes meaningfully to your overarching goals. This chapter delves into various ways to keep moving forward without losing sight of the future, emphasizing the dynamic nature of personal growth and the importance of flexibility in goal-setting.

In this chapter, readers will explore a diversity of methods and practices designed to maintain momentum on their path to self-improvement. From reflective practices like journaling and self-assessment to setting long-term goals using the SMART criteria, the chapter provides practical tools for staying motivated and resilient. Additionally, it will discuss the value of external supports such as accountability partners and peer groups, which can offer validation and fresh perspectives. Embracing adaptability in your plans ensures that you remain responsive to life's changes, turning potential obstacles into opportunities for further advancement. Through these comprehensive strategies, the chapter aims to equip you with the knowledge and skills needed to continuously thrive and look forward with confidence.

Reflection On Personal Growth

Reflecting on key milestones can play a crucial role in solidifying the changes in your life. It provides a clear view of the progress made and highlights how far you've come from where you began. Frequently, we advance without pausing to appreciate our journey. Acknowledging these milestones, regardless of their size, underscores the significance of every step taken toward personal growth.

To begin this practice effectively, consider maintaining a journal. Journaling about your experiences encourages deeper self-reflection and analysis of triggers that might have influenced your social anxiety. As Schroder (2018) suggests, journaling is not just about documenting what happened but also interpreting those experiences. When you write about your day-to-day interactions or significant events, focus on what transpired and on why it happened, and what you learned. This method helps bridge the gap between experience and understanding, fostering an insightful reflection that promotes personal growth.

Here are some tips for effective journaling:

1. Write with an open mind. Don't worry about grammar or structure at first. The goal is to capture your thoughts and emotions honestly.

2. Be detailed: Describe your experiences vividly to make them real when you review them later.

3. Reflect regularly: Make it a habit to review your journal entries. Reflecting on past entries can give you a more comprehensive view of your progress and areas needing improvement.

4. Use prompts: Questions like "What happened?", "Why did it happen?", and "What can I learn?" can guide your reflective practice (Schroder, 2018).

In addition to personal journaling, sharing your experiences with trusted friends or support groups can provide valuable perspectives and support. Sometimes, discussing your challenges and successes with others can offer new insights that you might not have considered. Trusted friends can validate your achievements and help you see your progress more clearly. Support groups, on the other hand, offer a community of individuals who may share similar experiences and struggles, providing a sense of belonging and mutual encouragement.

Regular and honest self-assessment is essential for recognizing both strengths and opportunities for improvement. This process involves introspectively examining your actions, feelings, and thoughts to understand what works well and what doesn't. Although self-assessment can be challenging due to the need for honesty and critical evaluation, its benefits are substantial. Identifying your strengths enhances confidence and reinforces positive behaviors and attitudes. On the other hand, recognizing areas for improvement enables you to take focused actions to address them.

To facilitate constructive self-assessment, consider these guidelines:

1. Set specific times for reflection: Allocate time daily or weekly to evaluate your progress and setbacks. Consistent practice ensures continuous learning and adaptation.

2. Be honest and gentle: While it's important to be truthful about your weaknesses, avoid harsh self-criticism. Constructive feedback should foster growth, not discourage it.

3. Ask probing questions: Inquire about the why and how of your emotions and actions. For instance, reflect on why a particular social situation made you anxious. What were the triggers? How did you handle it? What could you do differently next time?

4. Track your progress: Document your assessments over time to see patterns and trends. Celebrate improvements and strategize on overcoming persistent challenges.

Incorporating these practices into your routine helps build a robust framework for ongoing personal development. Reflecting on milestones ensures you acknowledge and appreciate your journey's progress, which is essential for motivation and self-esteem. Journaling offers a private space for deep reflection and understanding while sharing with others provides external validation and support. Regular self-assessment keeps you aligned with your goals and promotes a balanced view of your strengths and areas needing improvement.

Setting Long-Term Goals

Establishing a vision for the future through setting achievable long-term goals is crucial for personal growth beyond overcoming social anxiety. By focusing on continuous improvement, individuals can maintain their progress and stay motivated. One effective way to achieve this is by utilizing the SMART criteria (Specific, Measurable, Achievable, Relevant, Time-bound) to set clear and actionable goals.

The SMART framework provides a comprehensive and structured approach to goal setting, ensuring that each objective is clear, well-defined, and attainable. Specific goals offer clarity and prevent confusion or ambiguity, helping create precise targets to work toward. Measurable goals enable individuals to track their progress and assess their success over time, which is essential for maintaining motivation. Achievable goals ensure that the objectives are realistic and take into account one's skills, resources, and current situation. Relevant goals align with broader personal objectives, making sure that each step taken contributes meaningfully to overall development. Time-bound goals set clear deadlines, creating urgency and accountability that drive continuous effort and progress.

For instance, an individual aiming to improve their public speaking skills might set a specific goal of delivering a presentation at a local community event within the next six months. They can measure their progress by recording practice sessions and seeking feedback from peers. Ensuring the goal is achievable involves considering available resources, such as joining a public speaking club. Aligning this goal with broader personal development plans makes it relevant, and setting a six-month deadline makes it time-bound. Such structured goals facilitate steady advancement and maintain focus.

In addition to the SMART criteria, creating a vision board can serve as an engaging tool to visualize long-term aspirations. A vision board is a collage of images, quotes, and other items that represent one's goals and dreams. This creative activity encourages imagination and acts as a constant visual reminder of what one is striving to achieve. Placing the vision board in a prominent location ensures regular interaction, reinforcing motivation and commitment.

For example, someone aspiring to build stronger social connections might include pictures of group activities, inspiring quotes about friendship, and images that depict confidence and happiness. Seeing these visuals daily can instill a positive mindset and remind individuals of the joy and fulfillment that come with reaching their goals.

Another pivotal aspect of maintaining progress is identifying accountability partners. An accountability partner is someone who supports and motivates an individual by regularly checking in on their progress and offering constructive feedback. This relationship fosters a sense of responsibility and encourages follow-through, making it more likely for individuals to stay committed to their goals.

In practice, an individual working to overcome social anxiety could partner with a friend or mentor who is aware of their goals. Regular meetings or check-ins can be scheduled to discuss progress, challenges, and next steps. This partnership provides emotional support and practical advice, helping to navigate setbacks and celebrate successes. The social dimension of accountability adds an element of external validation and encouragement, enhancing overall dedication to personal growth.

While having a structured plan and accountability are essential, it is equally important to remain flexible with goals. Life is dynamic, and circumstances often change, necessitating adjustments to initial plans. Being open to modifying goals as needed enables adaptation and resilience, preventing discouragement when things don't go as planned.

For instance, if an individual set a goal to attend weekly social events but found it overwhelming, they could adjust the goal to attending bi-weekly or monthly events instead. This flexibility allows them to continue progressing at a manageable pace without feeling disheartened by setbacks. Recognizing that the journey may look different than originally envisioned fosters a growth mindset and adaptability.

Additionally, flexibility in goal setting means reassessing priorities as one evolves. Goals that were once relevant might become less significant over time. Regularly reviewing and adjusting goals ensures they remain aligned with current values and aspirations. This ongoing process promotes sustained development and prevents stagnation.

Integrating the SMART criteria, creating vision boards, establishing accountability partnerships, and maintaining flexibility enables individuals to set and achieve long-term goals effectively. These strategies promote ongoing development and sustain motivation. Such strategies aid in maintaining progress and help in building a resilient mindset for future challenges.

Reflecting on personal growth and setting long-term goals are crucial for maintaining progress and fostering continuous improvement. Embracing the journey of self-improvement involves regular self-assessment, journaling, and sharing experiences with trusted individuals or groups. These practices help recognize achievements, address challenges, and deepen self-understanding. Documenting and discussing experiences openly builds a supportive framework that nurtures ongoing development and resilience.

Looking ahead and setting clear, actionable goals is essential for sustained growth beyond overcoming social anxiety. Utilizing tools like the SMART criteria and vision boards helps keep efforts focused and inspired. Adding accountability partnerships provides additional support and motivation, ensuring commitment to your goals. Maintaining flexibility in goal-setting allows adaptation to changing circumstances, keeping the journey manageable and encouraging. Together, these strategies create a comprehensive approach to personal development, guiding individuals toward a fulfilling and confident future.

CONCLUSION

We've traveled this journey together, exploring the intricate world of social anxiety and uncovering practical ways to enhance our daily interactions. As we wrap up, let's celebrate the key takeaways from each chapter and envision how this newfound knowledge can transform your life.

We began by delving into the nature of social anxiety, identifying personal triggers, and exploring cognitive-behavioral techniques. These foundational insights have armed you with practical tools for real-life application. Identifying your triggers is like finding a guiding map through the labyrinth of anxiety, empowering you to navigate challenging social situations with greater ease and confidence.

Our journey continued with strategies to manage and reduce social anxiety in everyday scenarios. From deep breathing exercises to mindfulness practices, these tools are your immediate allies in moments of distress. Picture these strategies as pebbles creating ripples of calmness across the turbulent waters of anxiety, gradually making them second nature in your routine.

We then highlighted the transformative power of self-compassion and positive self-talk. Developing a kind inner voice can radically shift your perception of yourself and your interactions. Self-compassion allows you to forgive yourself for perceived flaws, fostering a healthier mindset. Instead of harsh self-criticism, embrace yourself as your own best friend, offering support and understanding through challenges.

Gradual exposure to feared situations was another key focus. This evidence-based approach emphasizes the power of facing fears incrementally. Breaking down seemingly insurmountable challenges into smaller, manageable tasks builds resilience and reinforces your ability to handle similar situations in the future.

We also covered the significance of strong communication skills. Effective communication alleviates misunderstandings and enhances connections with others. Practicing active listening, assertiveness, and empathy helps create meaningful interactions, boosting your confidence in social settings. Remember, communication is a skill developed over time—it's perfectly fine to make mistakes and learn from them.

The importance of a support system was a crucial aspect of our exploration. Friends, family, therapists, counselors, and support groups play vital roles in managing social anxiety. They offer a safety net during difficult times and celebrate your victories, no matter how small. Building and maintaining these connections reminds you that you are not alone; there's strength in seeking help and sharing your experiences.

Taking action based on the strategies presented is essential for change. Think of your comfort zone as a cozy bubble—stepping out might seem daunting initially, but it's essential for growth. Every small effort you make paves the way toward a more confident version of yourself. Each time you push beyond your limits, you expand the boundaries of what you once thought possible.

As we conclude, view overcoming social anxiety as a lifelong journey of growth and adaptation. Setting long-term goals and embracing change are integral to continual improvement. Regularly reflect on your progress and celebrate every step forward, no matter how minor it may seem.

Inspiration for continued growth can come from various sources—books, seminars, workshops, or conversations with those who share similar experiences. Learning doesn't stop here; the adventure of lifelong learning awaits, with each new experience offering an opportunity to refine your skills and broaden your horizons.

Carry the lessons and strategies from this book with you as you navigate life's social landscapes. Consider this conclusion not as an end but as the beginning of a more fulfilling and socially engaging life. Embrace each challenge with courage and view each setback as a temporary detour, not a permanent roadblock.

Your journey to better social interactions and an enhanced quality of life is uniquely yours. Trust in the process, be patient with yourself, and let growth unfold naturally. You have the tools, knowledge, and support to make meaningful changes. Take pride in your progress and look forward to the possibilities ahead.

As you close this book, let its wisdom guide you. Social anxiety may present obstacles, but with perseverance and the right approach, you can overcome them. Stay committed to your mental wellness, cherish the connections you build, and remember that small steps can lead to significant transformations.

Here's to a future filled with confident interactions, meaningful relationships, and a deeper understanding of yourself and others. May your journey be rich with growth, joy, and the courage to embrace each new day with renewed vigor.

Thank you for reading! If you enjoyed this book, please take a moment to leave a quick star rating for this author, and don't forget to check out the full library of interesting topics available in this author's library of work.

REFERENCES

Acoba, E. F. (2024, February 21). *Social support and mental health: the mediating role of perceived stress*. Frontiers in Psychology; Frontiers Media. https://doi.org/10.3389/fpsyg.2024.1330720

Anxiety Canada. (2023). *How to do Progressive Muscle Relaxation*. Anxiety Canada. https://www.anxietycanada.com/articles/how-to-do-progressive-muscle-relaxation/

Ankrom, S. (2024, February 16). *Need a Breather? Try These 9 Breathing Exercises to Relieve Anxiety*. Verywell Mind. https://www.verywellmind.com/abdominal-breathing-2584115

Baratz, A. (2024, May 3). *24 Social Anxiety Therapy Exercises to Try At Your Own Pace*. Besttherapists.com; Best Therapists. https://www.besttherapists.com/blog/social-anxiety-exercises

Bégin, C., Berthod, J., Martinez, L. Z., & Truchon, M. (2022, September 6). *Use of Mobile Apps and Online Programs of Mindfulness and Self-Compassion Training in Workers: A Scoping Review*. Journal of Technology in Behavioral Science. https://doi.org/10.1007/s41347-022-00267-1

Best Online Group Therapy of 2022. (n.d.). Verywell Mind. https://www.verywellmind.com/best-online-group-therapy-5215930

Browse Personal Stories | Anxiety and Depression Association of America, ADAA. (n.d.). Adaa.org. https://adaa.org/living-with-anxiety/personal-stories/all-stories

Centre for Clinical Interventions. (2019). Social anxiety self-help resources - Information sheets & workbooks. *Wa.gov.au*. https://www.cci.health.wa.gov.au/Resources/Looking-After-Yourself/Social-Anxiety

Comprehends. (2023, March 9). Virtual group therapy for adults struggling with anxiety - Mental health therapist in NYC. *Mental Health Therapist in NYC*. https://comprehensivecounselinglcsw.com/virtual-group-therapy-for-adults-struggling-with-anxiety/

Cuncic, A. (2018). Change your thoughts, reduce your social anxiety. *Verywell Mind*. https://www.verywellmind.com/what-is-cognitive-restructuring-3024490

Cuncic, A. (2019). Chill out: How to use progressive muscle relaxation to quell anxiety. *Verywell Mind*. https://www.verywellmind.com/how-do-i-practice-progressive-muscle-relaxation-3024400

Cuncic, A. (2024, February 12). 7 active listening techniques for better communication. *Verywell Mind*.

https://www.verywellmind.com/what-is-active-listening-3024343

Cohen, L. (2016). CBT strategies to overcome social anxiety. *National Social Anxiety Center*. https://nationalsocialanxietycenter.com/cognitive-behavioral-therapy/social-anxiety-strategies/

CNN. (n.d.). After years of debilitating social anxiety, a special tool changed my life. *CNN*. https://www.cnn.com/2022/04/01/health/social-anxiety-cognitive-behavioral-therapy-benefits-wellness/index.html

Cuncic, A. (2020, November 13). The best self-help strategies for social anxiety disorder. *Verywell Mind*. https://www.verywellmind.com/coping-with-social-anxiety-disorder-3024836

Cognitive Behavioral Therapy Los Angeles. (2020). CBT treatment for social anxiety disorder and social phobia. *Cognitive Behavioral Therapy Los Angeles*. https://cogbtherapy.com/cbt-for-social-anxiety-disorder

Drageset, J. (2021, March 12). *Social Support* (G. Haugan & M. Eriksson, Eds.). PubMed; Springer. https://www.ncbi.nlm.nih.gov/books/NBK585650/

Doyle, A. (2020, September 17). *List of Verbal Communication Skills Employers Seek*. The Balance. https://www.thebalancemoney.com/verbal-communication-skills-list-2059698

Gilboa-Schechtman, E., & Shachar-Lavie, I. (2013, December 31). *More than a face: a unified theoretical perspective on nonverbal social cue processing in social anxiety.* Frontiers in Human Neuroscience. https://doi.org/10.3389/fnhum.2013.00904

Felman, A. (2020, October 7). Social anxiety disorder: Causes, symptoms, and treatment. Www.medicalnewstoday.com. https://www.medicalnewstoday.com/articles/176891

Fletcher, J. (2019, February 12). *4-7-8 breathing: How it works, benefits, and uses.* Www.medicalnewstoday.com. https://www.medicalnewstoday.com/articles/324417

Hartzell, S. (2021, May 22). *Overcoming Anxiety and Panic Disorder - Stephen Hartzell - Medium.* Medium; Medium. https://stephenhartzell.medium.com/overcoming-anxiety-and-panic-disorder-7fff511f4c2f

Hernandez, D. R. (n.d.). *20 smart goals to become more confident and achieve more in life. Efficiency and Organization.* Retrieved from https://efficiencyandorganization.com/planning-%26-preparing/f/20-smart-goals-to-become-more-confident-and-achieve-more-in-life

Hofmann, S. G., Grossman, P., & Hinton, D. E. (2011, November). *Loving-kindness and compassion meditation: Potential for psychological interventions.* Clinical Psychology Review. https://doi.org/10.1016/j.cpr.2011.07.003

How to Practice Exposure Therapy for Social Anxiety & Worksheets (PDF). (2024, March 26).

https://www.simplypsychology.org/exposure-therapy-for-social-anxiety.html

How to Set Professional Goals for Yourself (With 11 Examples). (n.d.). Purdue Global. https://www.purdueglobal.edu/blog/careers/setting-professional-goals-with-examples/

Kaczkurkin, A. N., & Foa, E. B. (2018). *Cognitive-behavioral therapy for anxiety disorders: an update on the empirical evidence*. Dialogues in Clinical Neuroscience; Les Laboratoires Servier; ncbi. https://doi.org/10.31887/DCNS.2015.17.3/akaczkurkin

Luk, Q., Zhu, X., & Cheong, C. M. (2021, September 13). *Understanding the Difference Between Self-Feedback and Peer Feedback: A Comparative Study of Their Effects on Undergraduate Students' Writing Improvement*. Frontiers in Psychology. https://doi.org/10.3389/fpsyg.2021.739962

Martin, E. I., Ressler, K. J., Binder, E., & Nemeroff, C. B. (2009, September). *The Neurobiology of Anxiety Disorders: Brain Imaging, Genetics, and Psychoneuroendocrinology*. Psychiatric Clinics of North America; National Library of Medicine. https://doi.org/10.1016/j.psc.2009.05.004

Mayo Clinic . (2021, June 19). *Social anxiety disorder (social phobia) - symptoms and causes*. Mayo Clinic; Mayo Clinic. https://www.mayoclinic.org/diseases-conditions/social-anxiety-disorder/symptoms-causes/syc-20353561

Mind Tools Content Team. (2022). *MindTools | Home.* Www.mindtools.com. https://www.mindtools.com/ax3c2aw/celebrating-achievement

National Institute of Mental Health. (2022). *Social anxiety disorder: More than just shyness.* National Institute of Mental Health; National Institute of Mental Health. https://www.nimh.nih.gov/health/publications/social-anxiety-disorder-more-than-just-shyness

Northup, G. (2023, August 2). *Communication skills: Definitions and examples | indeed.com.* Indeed.com. https://www.indeed.com/career-advice/resumes-cover-letters/communication-skills

Overcoming low self-esteem: My story & tips. (2020, May 31). Notes by Alice. https://notesbyalice.co.uk/overcoming-low-self-esteem/

Pulapaka, S. (2023, April 6). *Self development through reflective practice.* Medium. https://medium.com/@shilpa.ukau/self-development-through-reflective-practice-75cd36bbd2ff

Philp .D, K. G. (2023, June 20). *How to Overcome Social Anxiety: 8 Techniques & Exercises.* PositivePsychology.com. https://positivepsychology.com/social-anxiety/

Ramani, S., Könings, K. D., Ginsburg, S., & van der Vleuten, C. PM. (2019, February 19). *Feedback Redefined: Principles and Practice.* Journal of General Internal Medicine. https://doi.org/10.1007/s11606-019-04874-2

Raypole, C. (2021, September 17). *Cognitive Behavioral Therapy (CBT) for Social Anxiety: How It Works.* Healthline. https://www.healthline.com/health/anxiety/social-anxiety-disorder-cognitive-behavioral-therapy

Reid, C. (2023, August 4). *The Power of Celebrating Small Wins and Their Positive Impact on Life.* Know Thyself, Heal Thyself. https://medium.com/know-thyself-heal-thyself/the-power-of-celebrating-small-wins-and-their-positive-impact-on-life-f2fd17c3dc51

Riopel, L. (2019, June 14). *The importance, benefits, and value of goal setting.* Positive Psychology. https://positivepsychology.com/benefits-goal-setting/

Rose, G. M., &; Tadi, P. (2022). S*ocial Anxiety Disorder.* PubMed; StatPearls Publishing. https://www.ncbi.nlm.nih.gov/books/NBK555890/

University of Massachusetts Global. (2020, April 6). *How Setting Effective Goals Can Improve Organizational Performance.* Www.brandman.edu. https://www.umassglobal.edu/news-and-events/blog/how-to-measure-organizational-performance

Sawchuk, C. (2017, May 17). *Fear of public speaking: How can I overcome it?* Mayo Clinic. https://www.mayoclinic.org/diseases-conditions/specific-phobias/expert-answers/fear-of-public-speaking/faq-20058416

Schroder, G. (2018, November 9). *Reflective Journaling as an approach to life*. Journaled Life. https://journaledlife.com/reflective-journaling/

Schuman-Olivier, Z., Trombka, M., Lovas, D. A., Brewer, J. A., Vago, D. R., Gawande, R., Dunne, J. P., Lazar, S. W., Loucks, E. B., & Fulwiler, C. (2020). *Mindfulness and behavior change*. Harvard Review of Psychiatry. https://doi.org/10.1097/HRP.0000000000000277

Selby. (2023, August 22). *Developing Situational Awareness: How to Improve Your Social Interactions | Everyday Speech*. Everyday Speech. https://everydayspeech.com/blog-posts/general/developing-situational-awareness-how-to-improve-your-social-interactions/

Segal, J., Smith, M., Robinson, L., & Boose, G. (2023). *Nonverbal Communication and Body Language*. HelpGuide. https://www.helpguide.org/articles/relationships-communication/nonverbal-communication.htm

Setting Goals for 2024 (With Examples). (n.d.). Www.betterup.com. https://www.betterup.com/blog/setting-goals-for-2023

Sherin, J. E., & Nemeroff, C. B. (2011, September). *Post-traumatic stress disorder: the neurobiological impact of psychological trauma*. Dialogues in Clinical Neuroscience; Les Laboratoires Servier. https://www.ncbi.nlm.nih.gov/pmc/articles/PMC3182008/

South Jersey Coping Clinic. (2024, March 24). How group therapy can help manage social anxiety. *South Jersey Coping Clinic*. https://southjerseycopingclinic.com/how-group-therapy-can-help-manage-social-anxiety/

Stanborough, R. J. (2020, February 4). *How to change negative thinking with cognitive restructuring*. Healthline. https://www.healthline.com/health/cognitive-restructuring

Tennant, K., Butler, T. J. T., & Long, A. (2023, September 13). *Active Listening*. Nih.gov; StatPearls Publishing. https://www.ncbi.nlm.nih.gov/books/NBK442015/

www.ingramcontent.com/pod-product-compliance
Lightning Source LLC
Chambersburg PA
CBHW071032240526
45469CB00006BD/2180